Innovation Stories from India Inc: Their Story in Their Words

Innovation Stories from India Inc: Their Story in Their Words

Vijay Menon

B L O O M S B U R Y
NEW DELHI • LONDON • OXFORD • NEW YORK • SYDNEY

First published in India 2017
This export edition published in 2020

ISBN 978-93-86432-69-8

Bloomsbury Publishing India Pvt. Ltd
Second Floor, LSC Building No.4
DDA Complex, Pocket C – 6 & 7, Vasant Kunj
New Delhi 110070
www.bloomsbury.com

Typeset by Manipal Digital Systems

Dedication

To Anitha, wife and Meghna, daughter. May the conversations be always interesting.

Preface

We constantly hear about innovation in Silicon Valley, Europe, South Korea, and other places. The stories about companies like Apple, IKEA, and Samsung are fascinating and interesting. But we don't get to hear too many stories about innovation in India Inc.

And yet, most of us can recall instances of being part of a creative flow. In my career as an engineer, journalist, and marketing leader, I have been part of several innovative initiatives. See the Appendix for a representative couple.

So in the summer of 2016, I went looking for stories of innovation at Indian workplaces. I met the leaders at a cross-section of Indian conglomerates, standalone companies, the Indian arm of MNCs, and startups. Over one-to-one conversations, these business leaders told me stories of product, process, and management innovations in their companies.

This book is the result of that journey. The stories here are real-life examples of how companies in India have innovated to forge ahead. Barring one, each story is crafted in two parts: an introduction to set the context followed by the company's innovation story in its leader's words.

The storytellers are some of India Inc's finest business leaders and I've tried to retain their distinctive voice. To preserve authenticity, I transcribed the interviews, edited them into a narrative, and filled gaps with supplementary research. I sent the resulting story to the interviewee in every case for a fact check. The result, I hope, is authentic and engaging.

So find a quiet spot, put your phone on silent, and turn the page. Fascinating journeys await.

Acknowledgements

A book like this that involved meeting several business leaders was always going to be challenging. Getting past the gate keepers was difficult with rare exceptions. So I'm deeply thankful to everyone who made the book possible: the leaders for their courtesy, time, and candidness; the corporate communication teams and executive assistants for setting up the meetings and vetting the resulting story; friends who helped with a contact or a suggestion; and my family, who were always patient sounding boards and critics. A big thank you also to Nitin Valecha and the team at Bloomsbury, without whom, of course, this book would have never been published.

In addition to the people named in the stories, these are the people, in alphabetical order, who helped make the book possible. Thank you. I'm very grateful.

A G Pandu
Akshatha TN
Anand Halve
Antaash Sheikh
Arjun Mukundan
Arup Mukherjee
Ashmita Pillay
Aviral and Aparna Khandelwal
C Vinayaraghavan
Calvin Printer
Deepak Morada
Dilnaz Gilder
Dipika Mohil
Drs Ashwini and Chitra Setya

Jayanth Nanjappa
Lata Sharma
Madhavan Varadharajan
Manoj Menon
P V G Menon
Pani Nagaraja
Premila Vaz
Priyanka Jha
R Parthasarathy
Rakesh Sinha
Rathnam Subramanyam
Rita Srivastava
Ritu Kalia
Rowena Carneiro
Rubina D'Silva
Sarika Kapoor Chokshi
Sarmishta Nandakumar
Sheelika Ravishankar
Sherna D'Mello
Sonia Dhawan
Sreeram Venkiteswaran
Sriram Gopalakrishnan
Tanuj Kumar
Tenzin Dechen Deshar

Contents

Ratan Tata

Epic. That's the word that comes to mind when writing about Ratan Tata, chairman of Tata Sons, the holding company of the Tata group (FY16 revenue $103 billion) for twenty-one years from 1991 to 2012, and interim chairman from October 2016 to January 2017. Tata, a conglomerate of some 100-odd companies, is India's largest business group and active in a wide array of industries from fashion to steel to automotive to software.

Ratan Tata (born 1937), returned to India in 1962 after graduating from Cornell University with a degree in architecture and working briefly with a Los Angeles-based architecture firm. He joined the family business and spent several years rotating through different roles and companies before being appointed chairman in 1991.

The initial years of his stewardship were mostly spent in consolidating his position and overcoming resistance from the old order in group companies. The second decade of Tata's leadership was marked by several big-ticket acquisitions as the group expanded and globalized on the back of economic liberalization and a rapidly-growing Indian economy. The notable buys were $450 million for UK's Tetley Tea, Rs 1591 crore for India's VSNL, $365 million for Singapore's NatSteel, $11.3 billion for Anglo-Dutch steel maker Corus, $2.3 billion for vehicle maker Jaguar Land Rover, and $1 billion for US-based General Chemical Industrial Products.

Going by the numbers, the Tata group under Ratan Tata grew at a compounded annual growth rate of about 22 per cent in both revenue and profit, a creditable achievement by any standard in large groups. From a financial standpoint, his big decisions have had mixed results. The UK operations of Corus steel turned unviable when the commodity cycle turned and cheap Chinese imports flooded the market. His pet project, the Nano, promoted as the world's cheapest car, sells in very low volumes. But Jaguar Land Rover is doing very well and the software business is thriving.

But the numbers don't tell the full story. Ratan Tata strides the Indian business landscape like a colossus. The acquisitions of Jaguar Land Rover and Corus steel not only heightened Indian self-esteem, they also brought Indian companies and brands on the international stage. At home, the Nano car project fired public imagination; and Tata Consultancy Services (TCS), along with other software companies, made India the IT services outsourcing capital of the world.

Unlike many business groups, however, the Tatas don't seem particularly interested in being seen as a success only in financial terms. Ratan Tata, like the chairmen who preceded him in the nearly 150-year-old group, seemed happy to preside over a sprawling group of companies of which only a handful would be attractive to financial analysts. But the group companies employ over 660,000 people and are a part of India's ethos. With their company townships, long history of corporate social responsibility programmes, hospitals, educational institutions, and patronage of arts and culture, the Tatas are an institution as much as they are a business group.

Ratan Tata is a man of great charm and courtesy but like all empire builders, there is steel beneath the velvet. This is a man who has made big bets and succeeded and failed on a grand scale. After his retirement from Tata Sons in 2012, he seemed perfectly content to manage the Tata trusts, enjoy his leisure, and invest his personal money in causes and ventures that excited him. And just when everybody thought that Tata had hung up his boots, he returned for a brief spell as interim chairman of Tata Sons in 2016 to sort things out and select a new chairman when the incumbent was replaced by the board. It was one more chapter in an epic journey.

To my mind, Ratan Tata is quintessentially an architect who enjoys envisioning and designing soaring structures. It is hard not to wonder how much more he could have done had he built a more effective nuts and bolts second line to execute that vision even better.

Leader speak: Ratan Tata

When I came back from the US, I was put through a very traditional training programme at Tata Steel and later at Tata Motors (called

TELCO back then). It lasted three and a half years and I considered it a total waste of my time then. In retrospect, it gave me the opportunity to work shoulder to shoulder with the people in those plants.

But what I also remember from that time is the frustration of a young person who had ideas and could not go anywhere with them. Every time I tried to talk to somebody, they would tell me, 'We know what we're doing. Grow some white hair before telling us what to do.'

This was the complete opposite of what my first job had been like. After college, I worked for a company in the US that built test sites for rockets. It was a new area and so people listened to everyone. If you said you had an idea to do something better, they'd say, 'Okay, go do it.'

So one of the hindrances to innovation is when you are not given a chance to express yourself. That is more likely to happen in large companies whether they are in India or the US or anywhere else because large companies have a legacy and baggage from the past and vested interests who want to maintain status quo. But this resistance to change is perhaps more ingrained in India than in some other places.

So when I got to senior positions, I was always receptive to a younger guy coming and talking about his idea. Throughout my career in Tata, I have quietly mentored many young, not startups, but small engineering companies that became suppliers to us. I have done this even when my colleagues said we shouldn't do it because we would be encouraging them at our cost, and that it would result in quality problems, and so on.

In fact, the automotive supply chain for our passenger vehicles was built like that. A colleague and I went to Europe asking component manufacturers to set up shop in India because of the forthcoming car industry. A lot of new joint ventures with Indian entrepreneurs were created as a result. In other cases, we encouraged existing suppliers like Bosch and Lucas to enhance their presence here.

So we've helped many companies to set up in India. I was the one that said, 'Go ahead, we will give you that first order.' In some cases, there was grief; in some cases we had success. We had to do this because the competition, the Suzukis and the Hyundais and others, they brought their established supply chain to India and while they produced excellent work, this supply chain was specific to them and closed to new entrants like us. So we had to grow our own.

People often ask me why our cars do not compare in quality with the international brands in the Indian market. To be fair, we are not too far behind on many of the core attributes such as engine, fuel efficiency, and so on. Where we trail is in fit and finish and final build quality.

I don't want to sound defensive but I would say the difference in quality between us and the others boils down to the quality of the supply chain. A passenger car has over 2500 distinct parts and can have over 100 suppliers making components and parts. We built a supply chain from scratch and encouraged small enterprises to set up and grow with us. The issue is that it will take some time for these suppliers to mature and come up to the quality standards of international suppliers such as Bosch or a Heller or a ZF.

The rigour that a foreign car manufacturer applies on suppliers is, I would have to say, very different from the level of rigour that that we bring to the table. Secondly, we still don't have the ability to wrestle with costs of the supply chain like our foreign counterparts do. We are getting better at both of these, but I would say we are still a little away from the level of rigour that we need to be at.

We see this difference in maturity levels of the supply chain even within the Tata group companies. In companies that manufacture products with comparatively less localization, for example, in Titan which makes highly successful watches but uses a fair amount of imported components, the finished product is world-class.

But in the case of vehicles, where the level of indigenization is very high, the quality of the finished product can be significantly affected by, say, a poor gearbox or a tyre or a switch or a headlamp or any one of the hundreds of parts that are made by local suppliers. We need to do a better job of ensuring high quality throughout that supply chain. We could have taken the easy route and sourced parts from established international suppliers. But that would have raised the cost, and in any case, our intent is to build a car that is as *Indian* as possible. It will take time to get to the standards of a Toyota or a Honda.

Let me extend the argument the other way. Consider the indigenous aircraft industry. An aircraft is far more complicated to build than a car and HAL (Hindustan Aeronautics Ltd.) has most of the technology and expertise needed to build one. But is the final product quality of their aircraft comparable to the big brands overseas? They have some way to go. Not because they don't have the skills. But because it takes time to develop that maturity in the supply chain to manufacture to the best-in-the-world standards.

This in turn, raises the question: *how can large companies create conditions that nurture innovation?* There are sufficient examples of Indian companies producing world class products and many of them tend to be relatively small and promoter-driven. Most entrepreneurs would say that the most exciting phase of their lives was when they were hands-on in their business and were personally involved in the creation and manufacture of their products.

But as companies grow, you have to delegate and as intervening layers grow between management and the final product, you need to develop systems and processes to maintain and retain excellence.

There are many ways to do this. For example, we have a simple system in Tata Motors that has been in place for decades. There is a suggestion box in the factory where people on the shop floor can suggest an improvement, get it vetted by a committee of peers and supervisors, and have it implemented in the plant. If the suggestion results in tangible gains, we share the profits with that person. It is our own version of Skunk Works.

I also think that companies, even large ones, are now more open to ideas than say, the time when I started working. Today you have more managers who say, 'Go ahead, try it out.' It is easier now than before to develop an idea inside a company if the company thinks that the idea is worth pursuing.

But the exciting change that has happened in recent years is that even if your company is not interested in pursuing your idea, now you have an external environment where it is possible to get some funding to start your own little venture to develop your idea.

I'm not saying it is easy or that you will not struggle initially, but the environment today is more conducive to entrepreneurs than before. There is this sprinkling of venture capital, the banks are a little more open, and there is an eco culture that says it is okay to take some risk.

In fact, the little bit of angel investing that I do is a good illustration of this change. When I see a young person with an idea or a dream wanting a little help, I am reminded of my younger days when people were not that receptive to new ideas. And so I try to back that person with my personal money. There are others like me and this was not the case earlier. This is something new in India.

But we still have a while to go before we get to funding large disruptive startups. The money for that will still need to come from outside. I'm not sure companies like Flipkart or Snapdeal could have ever grown to the size they have without someone like Tiger Global or SoftBank putting up the money. Sure, it helped that investors had the Amazon example to compare with when they evaluated Indian e-commerce companies. But how many Indian investors would have the risk appetite to fund startups at that scale?

The willingness to take risk is still low in India compared to the ability of a potential investor to recognize a disruptive technology, and bankroll it, and support it in, for example, the US. It's not high in Japan. It's not high in Singapore. But it's very high in the US. It's very high in China also because they are entrepreneurs by nature and because the government provides enormous support. The government in China is keen to embrace innovative and disruptive technologies .

But funding innovation is only one part of the issue. For an innovation to succeed, we also need to develop excellence in execution. We still have some way to go there. From what I've seen in our own companies and in many companies across India, we definitely need to reach a standard of operations and quality that we don't have today. We have to build the requirement, the criteria, and the testing capability to ensure that anything that is made in our supply chain meets standards higher than what we accept today.

When I look at our manufacturing plants and some of our multinational competitor's manufacturing plants, I see a distinctly different DNA. This can and does pose a significant threat. Customers will naturally gravitate towards products that are better made and longer lasting.

It will not be easy to reach this level of excellence. In countries like Germany or Japan, there is a discipline that demands a high standard of work from everyone. China did not have such a culture but has built the rigour into its industry to an amazing degree just like Japan did after the war.

We have to develop such a culture in India. We need to build in recognition for quality and excellence. That is still the missing piece in our innovation journey.

Godrej Group

The Godrej group (FY16 group revenue $4 billion) started in 1897 when Ardeshir Godrej started a company that manufactured locks. In the 120 years since then, the group has expanded into making many different products and offering services from consumer goods and durables to property, technology, agri-products, chemicals, and retail.

Adi Godrej (born 1942), chairman of the Godrej group, is a precise man. This is perhaps to be expected from a man with a bachelor's and master's degree from the famously rigorous MIT Sloan School of Management. When I called his office to schedule a meeting, his assistant asked me to email the brief. A few minutes later, she called and connected me to Godrej. He asked a couple of questions to clarify the brief, described how he'd like to respond, and set up the meeting at his office in Vikhroli. It was that professional and simple. At the meeting, Godrej was fully prepared. He outlined the four themes that his management team has implemented across group companies and explained how he thinks that has enabled innovation and growth. After the interview, he put me on to Rakesh Sinha, the head of global supply chain at Godrej Consumer Products, to fill in the details.

Leader Speak — Adi Godrej

In 2011, we set ourselves a rolling 10 x 10 growth target. This means that we would work to grow our group revenues on a rolling basis, both through organic growth and acquisitions, to be ten times bigger in ten years at any point of time. So in ten years, we would expect our group revenues to grow to $40 billion from the current $4 billion.

The 10 x 10 growth target means that we have set ourselves a goal of growing at 26 per cent on a compounded annual basis. That is a stiff target for any established business, more so in a difficult economic environment. I'm reasonably confident we'll maintain that growth rate. We've been on track, more or less, for the last few years. My confidence stems from the fact that we have put in place systems and processes to identify emerging opportunities in the market and to take advantage of those opportunities rapidly.

I'm particularly happy about three initiatives that we think are unusual and have helped us grow and deliver excellent shareholder returns consistently. These initiatives are EVA (economic value added), Theory of Constraints, and the 3 x 3 acquisition strategy.

Economic Value Added

Economic value added (EVA) is a measure of a company's financial performance based on the residual wealth calculated by deducting its cost of capital from its operating profit, adjusted for taxes on a cash basis. EVA champions the idea that a business is only profitable when it creates wealth and returns for shareholders. EVA requires performance above a company's cost of capital. Compared to other performance indicators, we find EVA useful because it shows how and where a company created wealth, through the inclusion of balance sheet items. This forces us to be aware of assets and expenses when making managerial decisions.

In 2001, we implemented EVA at four companies: Godrej Consumer Products, Godrej Properties, Godrej Industries, and Godrej Agrovet. We have seen significant value creation as a result, year after year. We use EVA to evaluate several business decisions such as acquisitions, capital expenditure, and make-versus-buy. In fact, all acquisitions done by Godrej Consumer Products over the last decade have all been evaluated to check whether they would be EVA accretive. When we set up a new factory or purchase new equipment, we always ensure that the decision is EVA positive. Prior to EVA, we used performance metrics such as net present value and internal rate of return for evaluating capital expenditure decisions but have found that EVA is a better measure.

We also follow what we call PLVR or performance linked variable remuneration for managers, and other non-unionized employees. PLVR is tightly linked to the increase in annual EVA of the business — higher the incremental economic value added, higher the variable remuneration. There is no upper limit. Since everyone's PLVR is linked to a common metric, there is great alignment between individual efforts and business results as a whole. PLVR typically forms 10 per cent to 30 per cent of the annual remuneration of employees. In exceptionally good years, the variable component can exceed the fixed component of remuneration, sometimes even by multiples. The good thing about PLVR is that every additional rupee of EVA generated by the business leads to additional payout for employees without any upper cap.

Theory of Constraints

The second important practice we have implemented in the group is the Theory of Constraints. The Theory of Constraints is a methodology for identifying the most important limiting factor, or constraint, that stands in the way of achieving a goal and then systematically improving that constraint until it is no longer the limiting factor. It was introduced and popularized by Eliyahu Goldratt in his 1984 book, *The Goal*.

We implemented the Theory of Constraints in 2004 when Dr Goldratt extended his practice to India and selected one company in each major industry to implement it. Godrej Consumer Products was the preferred company in the FMCG space. At Godrej Consumer products, we have implemented the Theory of Constraints across all our manufacturing facilities in India and at several facilities abroad. We have also implemented it in the demand fulfillment process to improve customer service levels.

The Theory of Constraints dynamically aligns all product supply processes such as procurement, manufacturing, and distribution to consumer demand. In practice, this means that unlike most consumer product companies, we do not forecast demand or stock excess inventory in anticipation of consumer demand. We just replenish stocks as needed.

This is a revolutionary approach and works by setting dynamic inventory buffers at various stock points. These buffers across the entire supply chain are used to move finished goods based on consumer demand. The processes in the Theory of Constraint ensure that stocks depleted as a result of servicing demand are replenished on a daily basis to ensure that we don't miss out on servicing any consumer demand.

This approach has significantly improved our service levels. Prior to implementing the Theory of Constraints, our service levels (measured as the availability of products in the stores) were in the low eighties. It is now running at 98 per cent, which is well above the industry benchmark of 92 per cent and the best-in-class of figure of 95 per cent. We have also brought down the inventory carried by our distributors by 60 per cent. We are now extending the Theory of Constraints framework to all our international acquisitions and are seeing significant benefits as we complete the first phase of implementation.

At a strategic level, the Theory of Constraints allows us to maintain a very low working capital. In fact, we work with a negative working capital at Godrej Consumer Products since we only replenish products on demand and do not lock up capital in inventory. As a result, we produce a lot of surplus and this is ploughed back into the business, notably for acquisitions.

3 x 3 acquisition strategy

A third important component of our strategy is acquisitions. Our acquisition-based growth has been mainly in the developing world and in areas where we are very strong. For example, Godrej Consumer Products is very strong in the bottom-of-the-pyramid market. There are tremendous opportunities in this segment. In India, for instance, there are only three categories of packaged branded products that are fully penetrated — soap, detergents, and matchsticks. Every family uses them in one form or another. Everything else is under-penetrated. That means there is great scope to increase the number of products that you can offer to families, as long as they are of good quality and affordable.

Godrej Consumer Products has made twelve acquisitions over the last decade. The acquisitions are in line with what we call our 3 x 3 strategy. We focus on the three product categories: personal care, hair care, and home care; and in three geographies: Asia, Africa, and Latin America. All these product categories are underpenetrated and all three geographies are high growth regions with markets that are similar to India.

We run Godrej Consumer Products as a multi-local organization, which is very different from the way a traditional MNC is structured. We tend to acquire companies that are well run and that have leading brands in their respective markets. Once we acquire them, we retain the acquired company's management team and support them with improved processes in planning, finance, new product development, HR, supply chain, and so on.

We also bring together ideas from across our product portfolio and geographies to produce world-class products relevant to our audiences. Of course, it depends on how one defines the term 'world-class'. It doesn't make sense for us to make products that are expensive and only affordable by the affluent. We make top-notch products that can be purchased by almost anyone.

Let me illustrate this with three examples. First, we make a one-rupee mosquito repellent called the Good Knight Fast Card. It's inexpensive and in the first year of its launch, we sold over one billion pieces. The Fast Card burns for only three minutes and replaces mosquito coils on occasions when you don't want to burn a coil for several hours or you don't want to be exposed to smoke for a long time. Second, we are leaders in manufacturing hair color in many countries and this is the result of learning from different geographies and bringing many ideas together. Our Crème hair color, priced at thirty rupees and delivered in a sachet, competes with products that are priced four times higher. Third, we make a small refrigerator that is very inexpensive and very popular in rural areas where, among other things, it is used to store and preserve medical supplies.

I could go on. The point is that at Godrej, we believe we have put in place processes that foster an environment that spurs and nurtures innovation and growth. Because of our 10 x 10 growth goal, because of strategies such as 3 x 3, because of practices like the Theory of Constraints, and because of performance measures like EVA, we are able to attract good talent, offer them challenging work, and reward high performers exceptionally.

TVS Group — Sundram Fasteners

The TVS group (FY16 revenue $6.5 billion) is an automotive conglomerate of more than fifty companies specializing in the manufacture of two-wheelers, three-wheelers, and auto components and parts. They also own and run auto dealerships and trucking operations, and manage India's largest multinational logistics company.

TVS started in 1911 as a rural bus service in Tamil Nadu. Its city bus service in Madurai was famous for punctuality. It was said you could set your watch by the TVS bus. Known for a paternalistic style of management, almost all the group companies are headed by family members who maintain a low profile and follow a conservative management style.

Suresh Krishna (born 1936), the chairman of the TVS group, and chairman and managing director of Sundram Fasteners Ltd (FY16 revenue Rs 3261 crore, $500 million), India's biggest manufacturer of industrial fasteners, embodies the TVS culture. A student of literature, educated at the universities of Madras, Wisconsin, and Munich, Krishna has run his company for over fifty years without losing a single day to industrial unrest. He seamlessly combines Japanese quality practices with old-fashioned Indian patriarchy and is equally at ease talking about manufacturing, management, and Hindu philosophy.

Leader Speak - Suresh Krishna

The TVS Group is over 100 years old and the group companies are run by very diverse people in a manner they see fit. So I would be at a loss to talk about any overarching innovation themes across the whole group. Instead, I would like to discuss one aspect of innovation in my company, Sundram Fasteners, that is close to my heart and which I believe is largely neglected in India.

I'm talking about industrial relations. Indian companies have always had problems with labour. They are mostly disconnected from labour and leave it to professional managers. They almost seem to take it as inevitable that there will be stoppages of work due to unrest, strikes, and other disruptions now and then.

At Sundram Fasteners, we haven't lost a single day due to labour unrest in the 50 years of our existence. Not one. Not just in Chennai but across all our plants in Tamil Nadu, Uttarakhand, and China. Not even during countrywide general strikes and *bandhs*.

I know we are extremely fortunate. But I also believe that one of the reasons we have been fortunate is that we think that industrial relations is very important and we have a unique and very Indian approach to labour management. While our approach to labour may seem difficult to replicate, it can be done if you put your heart and soul to it.

When my father ran the TVS bus service in Madurai in the 1940s, the company employed people from the nearby villages. They were trained by my father and in time they became conscious of quality, they learned the importance of being punctual, they learned how to repair a bus, how to drive safely, why it was important to be polite to passengers, and so on.

There was one really important thing that my father did. After the day's business, all the buses would return to the depot at midnight. Once a month or so, my father would go to the depot and address all the workers when the buses returned. It was called the 'midnight shift talk'. Everyone would be there. My father would talk about many things. He would talk to the staff about how the company was doing, about what was happening in the country and the world, about things that affected their lives. Nothing was barred. He did this in all the years that he ran the business. I attended a few of these talks as a boy.

When I started Sundram Fasteners in 1966, I replicated this practice. I do this in each of our locations. I ask all the managers and staff to gather around. Everybody from the president to the lowest ranked employee attends and we meet on several occasions — New Year Day, bonus paying days, Founder's Day, and so on.

I talk to the staff about many things, like my father did before me. I tell them about the company's balance sheet. I tell them about what is happening in the world. I tell about the competition, about new product development, about the philosophy of the company—everything. I have no secrets because there is nothing to hide in the company. And since the message comes from the chairman, there is no ambiguity. Nobody can misinterpret the message. Everybody hears the same thing. And I always call a spade a spade.

Over the years, over countless such conversations, you develop something very important. Trust. Trust between labour and management cannot be mandated, cannot be bought, cannot be legislated. It can only be earned. And once the trust is established, there is no question of the workers at any point of time distrusting the management's decisions. So whenever I say something, it is taken at face value. There is no second-guessing; none at all.

This trust is the reason we haven't lost a single day to industrial unrest. Not even when our group companies were affected. Even during countrywide general strikes, our workers have jumped the fence and come to work in all three shifts because they think it is morally wrong to betray the trust.

This did not happen because of some magic of management. This happened because everyone in the company feels himself to be a stakeholder. I've thought about how this has come to be and I believe it has evolved out of four principles.

The first is the vision for the company. What is the vision? Where should the company go? This vision is not my vision. It is culled from various things that I gather from our customers, from our management, from labourers, from people who are working in the company everywhere. The vision is derived from all of this.

The second is the communication of the vision. You have to communicate, communicate, and keep on communicating till the vision becomes a company vision. It's no longer my vision. Every worker, every manager, every supervisor owns that vision. I never tyre of communicating. In fifty years I must have been part of 200 or more communication sessions. They last for about thirty to forty minutes and in these sessions I speak on all kinds of subjects, not just business. Nothing is barred.

The third principle is that once you have communicated and reiterated the vision, you set milestones for the company. Where should the company be two years or three years from now? This is important because it is very difficult to work in an amorphous environment. We need a clear goal of where exactly we are going. So we set milestones. The milestones are stretched, but not unachievable.

And that brings us to the fourth principle. The milestones should be reachable because everybody wants to feel like a winner. It is very important that people feel they've achieved something. So we set milestones that stretch people but do not strain them to the point where the target is not reachable. So most of the time we pass the milestone and this creates a culture of winning. People look back and say, 'Yes, we did it!' That's important.

We've done this for the last forty to fifty years. We've set milestone after milestone and we've passed them one by one. I started doing this when the company had just twelve employees. Now I address 8,000 employees in various locations.

What we have achieved with this approach is that everyone in Sundram Fasteners believes that it is a winning organization. There is no such thing as defeat. If we don't cross a milestone this year, this is just a stepping stone for a win later. What this has done is to create a lot of energy in the company. If you were to ask someone how the company is doing, they'd most likely tell you we are doing just great.

Don't get me wrong; there will be the odd personal grievances. Someone didn't get a promotion or someone did not get enough of a raise; that's normal. But I am confident that the vast majority of the people in the company think that we are going in the right direction.

Let me illustrate this optimism with what I hear when people come and meet me when they retire. Most of our staff have a long tenure with us. So when they retire after 30 to 35 years of service, they request to see the chairman. I always agree.

When I meet them, I ask them about their health, about their housing, about their children, and so on.

They normally have good things to tell me. Their health and their family's health is looked after by the company. They normally say that they have built a house or bought a flat, sometimes more than one. They normally say their children are settled; the sons are employed, the daughters are married. More often than not these days, the daughters are employed too. We help by running computer classes and vocation training programmes for children of our staff and we provide scholarships to bright students.

You must remember that most of our staff—the workers, not managers, come from deprived backgrounds. As a young man, a person would have left his village with a few rupees in his pocket to earn a living. Now, after thirty years of service to the company, his house is fully paid for, his health is taken care of, and in most cases, his children are settled.

So what has happened over this person's working life is that he has raised himself and his family from near-poverty level to a middle-class lifestyle. And when this happens for 8,000 workers and their families, it is no small thing.

I have asked myself many times, what is the dharma that guides us? What is our dharma in running a company? Take a schoolteacher teaching mathematics. What is his dharma? To teach as well as possible, of course. But it doesn't stop there. Years later, maybe twenty years later, it is possible that a former student tells you that without that teacher, he would have never learnt mathematics so well. He may tell you that he loves mathematics only because of that teacher. Like a ripple, the schoolteacher's influence has spread far and wide.

So what is the dharma of Sundram Fasteners? I believe our dharma is to raise the standard of living of a person entering our workforce to an extent that he can in turn provide his family with opportunities that he never had as a child. Enabling that cycle of progress is our dharma.

For all of us in the company, the path to that increased level of prosperity and progress is through our work. It is about doing the job to the best of our ability, to the standards that our customers set for us. So in a very tangible way, work is worship.

People tell me this is a very patriarchal way of managing. They tell me that today's employees have no time for such philosophy. They tell me that people no longer have loyalty to a company, only to their aspirations.

Perhaps. I don't speak for others. I can only speak from my experience of running a company for fifty years without disruption.

If you say employees today have no time for our style of functioning, I have no quarrel with you.

But I do know that in my experience, young people look for a parental figure. This is how it was in the India that I know. We look up to elders and figures of authority for guidance. That doesn't change just because you wear a company uniform and work on the shop floor. A young apprentice looks for a loco parentis—be it his supervisor, his manager, or the chairman. They come with dreams in their eyes and if we can help them achieve some of those dreams, then we have succeeded as a company. We have employees who joined us as a machine operator and their children have gone on to become doctors, business leaders, researchers, and so on, in organizations in India and overseas.

Yes, size does make a difference in how personally connected you can be. When we were small, I knew everybody and their families. That is no longer the case but my way of working hasn't changed. I still talk to everyone, we still build a shared vision and set milestones, and we still grow through many small wins. This has been true from the time of our first plant with just twelve employees in Ambattur to now having plants in Padi, in Madurai, in Puduchery, in Hosur, in Uttarakhand. It has worked even in China where our employees have the same need for guidance as in India. Our managers in every location espouse the same philosophy and they communicate the same values. We weave in these values with all the modern management practices on the shop floor from Kanban to TQM to supply chain management.

And it works. We are routinely awarded and win accolades for our quality and excellence in manufacturing. We won the Supplier of the Year award for five years consecutively from General Motors, something they award only to a select few of their 30,000 suppliers. So there is no dichotomy between modern practices and our traditional values.

But there is no magic bullet. It has taken us decades to get here. We've always sought out demanding customers because in serving them, we grow by raising our level to do better. And we are able to do that again and again because there is a conviction in all of us that this is our dharma. If we are to elevate ourselves, if we are to improve our standard of living, if we are to give our children significantly better opportunities than what we had, we have to raise our level and do better all the time.

People say we are not aggressive enough. At industry conferences, people tell me TVS could have been much bigger. Perhaps. But we are comfortable with who we are. India offers many opportunities and we are growing and will continue to grow. But not at the cost of our dharma.

GE India Technology Centre

General Electric has over 5,300 researchers and engineers in India located across four technology centres in Bangalore, Hyderabad, Chennai, and Mumbai. The John F. Welch Technology Centre (JFWTC) in Bengaluru was set up in 2000 and is GE's first and largest multidisciplinary research and development centre outside the USA. JFWTC is a fifty-acre site that represents $220 million in investments. With co-located research and engineering teams from across GE businesses, the centre delivers innovative solutions for India and the world. It houses engineering teams from Healthcare, Transportation, Aviation, Power, Oil & Gas, Renewable Energy, Energy Connections and Digital. JFWTC also houses a GE Global Research Centre, one of nine such centres around the world, the others being located in China, Germany, Brazil, Israel, Saudi Arabia, and the USA. GE technologists in India have contributed to over 3,500 patent applications filed by the parent General Electric Company.

This story is based on interviews with Munesh G Makhija, chairman and managing director, GE India Technology Centre Pvt Ltd and chief technology officer, GE South Asia; several of his team members including Manoj Kumar, Anil Rajanna, Venkatarao Ryali, and Tenzin Deshar; and Shyam Rajan, the chief technology officer, India, of Wipro GE Healthcare. Munesh Makhija (born 1970), holds a master's degree in electrical engineering and an MBA, and joined GE in 2003 after ten years in the telecommunications industry. He has led development teams in Asia, Europe, and the USA.

Leader speak: Munesh Makhija

Over the 125 years of its existence, GE has reinvented itself many times. Innovation for us is not the goal; the goal is the outcome.

That outcome can be growth, productivity, speed, or any differentiation that we are trying to create for our products.

India is important to GE not only because it is home to some of our best technologists who work on products both for India and the world, but also because India is an important and large market for us.

There are three broad themes that define work at GE globally and India is very much at the centre of these themes: industrial to digital; local and global; and horizontal and vertical.

Industrial to digital

As a company, GE continuously evaluates and changes its portfolio of products and services to remain relevant to our markets and customers. Even as recently as eighteen months ago, GE was fifty per cent a financial services company. Over the next two years, we expect to have divested much of the financial services business to refocus on engineering products, and digital technology is changing the way we do things completely. India is at the cutting edge of this transition.

Our Brilliant Factory in Pune is a good example of this transition. This is a $200 million facility that was set up in 2015 to produce a variety of products from jet engine parts to locomotive components for different GE businesses—all under one roof. It's the first time that such a variety of products will be made in the same facility and this is only possible because of what we call a multi-modal capability. At the Pune factory, equipment and computers talk to each other over the internet in real time, share information, and make decisions to preserve quality, and prevent downtime. The production lines are digitally connected to supply, service, and distribution networks to maintain optimal production.

This is a completely new way of manufacturing things and what it does is to helps us reconfigure, forecast demand, and be more flexible. And the reason it works is because in a market like India, we export about half of the output but half of the output is done just for India. India may not have the critical mass if you focus on any one single vertical but it has critical mass when you aggregate across the verticals. So the constraints forced us to think differently and create this platform that doesn't exist anywhere else in the world. We are now replicating this in other geographies such as Africa, the Middle East, and Latin America.

Local and global

The second big theme that India is very much part of is our mix of local and global. Like every multinational company, GE needs to balance local and global aspirations in every location it operates in.

So we ask ourselves, what does it mean to be a local company? Sure, you can manufacture locally and you can source locally. But what does it mean from an innovation standpoint to be a local company?

For GE, it boils down to having the courage to unlearn. It is the ability to understand a local need and not to be blinded by what you have done elsewhere in the world to arrive at solutions that are best for that market and extend it to other markets. Let me illustrate with a few examples.

Affordable healthcare. In India, GE Healthcare develops affordable and accessible technologies to address four of India's critical healthcare areas— cardiology, oncology, maternal and infant health, and trauma. Addressing local challenges and specific user requirements, these solutions help improve access to quality healthcare through lower costs, portability, durability, effectiveness, and ease of use. Many of these technology solutions are developed in India and find application in over 100 countries around the world.

The story really began with an affordable ECG (electrocardiogram) machine that we developed in India in 2007. GE offers a range of high-end ECG systems but these are designed for major hospitals in urban centres and were too expensive for the small town and rural Indian clinics that were our target market for this product. Our goal was to bring down the cost of an ECG reading to about eight rupees, the price of a bottle of water at that time. That meant building an ECG machine for under $1000 when the cheapest machine in our portfolio anywhere in the world cost $2500. So there was no way we could have reduced cost by de-featuring an existing machine, by reducing the functionality to the bare minimum. That would have got us down to maybe half the existing price but not further.

So we started from scratch. Our teams went to small towns and rural clinics to get a sense of the environment in which these machines would operate and they came back with a bunch of insights. They found that the machines would need to operate with erratic power supply, with little service backup, and there would be no cardiologist to interpret the results.

So we improvised. We replaced the sophisticated analogue front ends that acquired data, filtered signals before digitizing it, and all of that. Instead, we used a simple analogue-to-digital converter with a digital signal processor. For power, we used lithium-ion technology used in mobile phones so that you could charge the batteries anywhere with the dirtiest of power. The innovation on the printer was even more dramatic. We have a centre of excellence in Germany that makes printers for all of GE's medical devices and they were trying to help us build a simple printer. That's when we discovered the solution literally under our noses—we simply adapted the mobile printers in use all over India by the police, the bus conductors, and in shops. Sure, we modified them to improve accuracy and reliability but we didn't reinvent the wheel. Somebody had figured it out before. And we loaded the machine with our database and algorithm developed over several years that could interpret an ECG reading and flag abnormalities.

The result was the MAC 400—a portable, battery-operated device with ECG interpretation capability. Above all, it was priced at $800, compared with other hospital-class units from GE Healthcare that range from $2,000 to $10,000. It was a breakthrough product and it enabled rural and low-income sections of the Indian population to access ECG for screening.

We've done this repeatedly in our affordable healthcare portfolio. Again and again, we have resisted the attempt to drive the cost down by de-featuring an existing product and simply used local inputs and ingenuity to build products that start out being developed for the local Indian market, but have evolved to become a rage in other developing markets and even in some developed markets.

Today, we have a portfolio of 28 affordable healthcare products that includes portable ECG machines, mobile x-ray equipment, baby warmers, ultrasound machines, and more. The latest is the Revolution ACTs—the first ever CT (computed tomography) designed, developed and manufactured in India. It is the result of four years of R&D by 75 GE researchers and engineers in collaboration with over 500 healthcare providers from urban as well as rural settings. This CT is 40 per cent cheaper than the imported, previous generation four-slice CTs and is opening a whole new segment of CT users in tier three and four towns in India.

Wind turbines. A third outstanding example of innovation out of India is in renewable energy. GE launched its first *for India* wind turbine in 2014, engineered specifically for the country's low wind speed conditions. The 1.7-103, which was designed and assembled in India, provides a 30 per cent increase in annual energy production compared to its predecessors. Today, GE Renewable Energy has over 1 GW generating capacity spread across five states in India.

GE's recent offering for the India market is the 2.3-116 wind turbine, launched along with Digital Wind Farm capabilities in March 2016.The 2.3–116 comes with enhanced control technology and safety features, including a new 94 metre tower height and the largest 116 metre diameter rotor in the country. It provides approximately 30 per cent more gross Annual Energy Production (AEP) over its predecessor, the 1.7-103.

Apart from hardware, the India team has also delivered a novel Digital Twin technology that is best-in-class in India to accurately forecast power generation from a wind farm. This was in response to the RRF regulation (Renewable Regulatory Fund) that the Government of India passed to make wind power more predictable. The team demonstrated that their self-learning algorithms, when applied to real wind farms, produced results that were five to seven per cent better than the best solution available in the market. GE's work was cited by the government in India and today this solution is deployed at five different sites in India.

Multiphase flow meter. But Indian ingenuity at GE goes far beyond just making products for emerging markets. Take the case of the multiphase flow meter that we are developing in India with the global GE Oil & Gas business team. This high accuracy multiphase flow meter is important in top-side, sub-sea, and refinery environments. An oilfield can have thousands of wells. When you dig in these wells, what comes out is a mixture of oil, water and gas and you want to know how much of each has come out. The methods that are available today are cumbersome and inaccurate and they take time. So if you are a large oil company with tens of thousands of wells to be sampled, you have a real problem. What we have done is to use multiple sensors and technologies and an intelligent algorithm so that the meter now provides volumetric flow rate measurement of individual phases (oil, water, gas) without separating them. GE has entered into an alliance with Chevron to commercialize the Safire flow meter. Today, the GE Safire 2.0 meter is deployed in the US and Canada. So this is a GE innovation out of India for the world.

Culture innovation

The third big GE theme that India is part of is what we call horizontal and vertical in human resource management. GE prides itself on being a great talent development organization. We spend a lot of money and effort in grooming both technical and managerial excellence, and the way we do it evolves continually.

By the way, and I get asked this a lot, we haven't had the famous (or infamous) rank and stack and cull the bottom 10 per cent appraisal system for a long time now. That went out at least ten years ago.

For the last forty or fifty years, we've had what we call EMS or employee management system. This is basically an annual appraisal mechanism to provide feedback and drive differentiation. Nothing much had changed in all that time. Sure, we had gone from a paper-based to an online system but the process was pretty much the same: you rate yourself, your manager rates you, you look at strengths, you look at areas of development, you set a goal for next year, and you were on your way.

We've now pretty much challenged everything about the EMS process to bring it in line with the changed environment. The changes are huge. First off, we've pretty much done away with annual goal setting and targets because things now change faster and you have to shape priorities and reshape priorities frequently and still deliver an outcome. So now, we all carry an app on our phones that enables us to seek and give, not feedback but insights to people so that they can get a 360-degree view of how they are doing at short intervals. It creates a dialogue that says, 'What is it that you are doing that's working? What needs to change? How can we move faster towards an outcome?' India is a great place to test and flesh out this process because of our size and because every business of GE is represented here.

Nestlé India

Nestlé India Ltd (FY15 revenue Rs 8175 crore, $1.25 billion) is the Indian arm of Nestlé, the $92 million food giant ranked 66 in the Fortune Global 500 list. Nestlé has been in India since 1912 and its brands, Cerelac, Nescafe, Kit Kat, EveryDay, and Maggi, among others, are household names. For over a hundred years, Nestlé went about its business quietly in India and even has a little ditty to celebrate its success: In a rice country we make noodles; in a tea country we sell coffee; in a sweets country we sell chocolates; in a freshmilk country we sell powder.

That complacency was shattered by an event that everyone in the company refers to as 'the crisis.' In April 2015, a government referral laboratory in Kolkata, following up on an initial report from Barabanki in Uttar Pradesh, reported excess lead in samples of Maggi, Nestlé's instant noodles brand that then commanded 63 per cent share of India's Rs 5000 crore noodle market. Following a public outcry, the product was pulled from the market and banned by the Indian government in June 2015. Nestlé insisted on the safety of its product and contested the ruling. In August 2015, the Bombay High Court overturned the government's ban. In November 2015, Maggi was relaunched after court-mandated tests. Various Maggi-related cases are still working their way through other Indian courts. Nestlé lost more than Rs 500 crore (US$77 million) over the ban, which forced it to destroy more than 37,000 tonnes of Maggi noodles.

Suresh Narayanan (born 1960), chairman and managing director of Nestlé India, was brought in to manage the crisis. Narayanan, whose slightly academic demeanor has not stopped him from implementing major sales and structural changes, has previously headed Nestlé units in Singapore, Egypt, and Philippines.

An alumnus of the Delhi School of Economics, Narayanan has attended executive programs at IMD Switzerland and the London Business School. At our meeting in the sinuous glass-clad Nestlé building in Gurgaon, Narayanan spoke about how the crisis has made the company innovate and execute faster. Amit Narain, the head of human resources says the company 'learned more in the five months of the crisis than in five years.' By June 2016, Maggi noodles had climbed back to a 57 per cent market share, a remarkable comeback indeed.

Leader speak: Suresh Narayanan

There is a lot of innovation that goes on at Nestlé within the boundaries of our quality and food safety guidelines. Our roots are in baby food, Cerelac, and that makes us fanatical about food safety. Our factories regularly win accolades and awards for hygiene, quality, safety, and community work. In fact, Nestlé as an organization is structured to insulate quality from the pressures of short-term business goals; so much so that my technical director has a dotted line reporting to me but a straight line to Switzerland. That's true in every country and this is to ensure that the country head cannot compromise quality to satisfy business exigencies. So when a laboratory in Barabanki said that our noodles were unsafe, it was a complete shock.

We are the world's biggest spender on R&D as a company and that is valorized in the science that goes into the products that we make.

We also have a clear philosophy: *think global and act local*. As long as you operate within quality boundaries, local leaders are given plenty of freedom to innovate.

Maggi Noodles is a great example of this decentralization. Not many people know that Maggi is a completely Indian innovation. We had something similar in Malaysia at the time but the noodle brand we introduced in India in 1983 was a local creation. It was a huge leap of faith because we were introducing noodles in a rice and wheat eating country. It says a lot about the long-term vision of Nestlé that in spite of Maggi being a dead loss for the first ten years, the company persevered. It recognized that food habits take a long time to change and of course, the rest is history. India is now world's biggest market for Maggi noodles. There are variants that are either manufactured in or exported to a handful of other markets but India is the biggest one for Maggi.

There are other product innovation success stories out of India. Take the case of Munch. Nestlé is big in wafers and Kit Kat is a big brand but Munch is a tropicalized variant that was created in India and has now spread to China, Middle East, and Africa.

Innovation demands a certain ability to stay the course. Nestlé is not a company that says, okay, let's give a project two or three years and shut it if it doesn't work. If we see a proposition with traction in terms of either brand, or association, or usage, or penetration going up over a period of time, the company is willing to invest in it for the long term.

So we nurse a portfolio of brands. Some are mature brands and we expect them to drive growth for an extended period of time. Some are a middle category of products that we need to tweak or invest in more to grow into giants. Then we have our nursery, which has all those brands that need a lot of support before they can grow.

Many of our new launches are in this last category: our Nestlé Grekyo brand of Greek yoghurt is a totally new concept in India. Nescafé Sunrise Insta-Filter is a product where we offer the South Indian filter coffee experience with a dry decoction. EveryDay Masala Fusion is a dairy whitener impregnated with a blend of spices so that you can enjoy an instant cup of masala tea.

We're even tweaking existing brands. We've introduced six new variants of Maggi called HotHeads. They have high levels of spice and they come in exotic flavors because young India loves to experiment. Who knew what peri peri was when we were growing up? But the kids today do and they like new tastes and new experiences. Hence the new flavours. Then there is Munch Nuts, a chocolate wafer with peanuts. And Nescafé Cappuccino ready-to-drink premixes, and so on.

In all, we've launched twenty-five new products or variants since the Maggi crisis. All of these are in the incubator. Some will gallop in the future; others will canter, some may die.

People ask me, what has changed? How did Nestlé suddenly acquire this pace? We've never had so many product launches in such a short time in the history of the company.

I think the answer to that is deeply rooted in the sense of purpose in this company and the values we have. On the face of it, nothing much has changed. In spite of the Maggi factories being shut down for five months affecting over 3,000 employees, we did not have any industrial unrest. No supplier left us. No vendor left us. No distributor left us. That tells you something about the trust we've managed to build in the community.

When we were beleaguered by accusations of bad quality, we checked and rechecked our supply chain, our production and quality processes, our training methods—everything. I don't think we came up short on anything that was of any significance. So the capability, the rigour, the processes were all still there. We didn't have to introduce anything drastically new.

But what did change was that we suddenly had a new sense of purpose, a mission. I think there was this burning desire to demonstrate that this was a company that not only produced safe and high-quality food but also was *seen* to produce safe and high-quality food.

When an organization has that strong a sense of purpose, people tend to drop whatever they're doing and focus on the big goal.

This was a new territory for us. Nestlé has never been a high-profile company. We like to live quietly. The crisis put us in the spotlight and we were definitely outside our comfort zone.

My message to everyone was, 'Okay, like it or not, we are in a spot. We can either feel sorry for ourselves; or we can treat this as a life crisis and come out stronger'. The choice was ours.

I've always believed that culture eats strategy for breakfast. Grandiose plans have their place but in a crisis, you need many small wins to sustain morale. At a macro level, getting Maggi back on the shelves and winning back our market share was important because it was one-fourth of our revenue.

But getting there needed a huge effort. We had to break that goal into winnable tasks. So we set ourselves a date for the launch of Maggi. We said we'd launch on the eve of Diwali 2015. That was just four weeks from the time the courts gave us permission to restart production.

Then we worked backwards and set up timelines that we would never have believed to be possible in normal times. It was a big step but I told the team to seize the moment. If we could pull this off, we would have set ourselves completely new benchmarks for the future.

So we crunched our timeframe. There was no scope for saying we need six weeks or eight weeks to do this or that. We did not have six week. We did not have eight weeks. We just had four weeks to launch.

So we looked at everything afresh. How could we shorten the internal approval cycle? What would it take to reduce a ten-day process to two days? Could we package faster? Could we transport faster? We put in place a core group of people across different businesses sponsored by me and some of my management committee members. We met almost on a daily basis to review and remove blocks. It was a very active intervention. People saw the senior management fully involved and that was a powerful catalyst.

At some level, this is a proud organization. We like to be low key but people have long tenures here and they take great pride in working at and belonging to Nestlé. So there was an intrinsic desire to prove something and everyone came together to make the launch successful. We relaunched, bang on schedule, on November 9.

I've used that energy to continue the surge. I went back to the teams and said, 'Okay, whatever we did in the four weeks to launch Maggi, let's do the same for the twenty-five other products'.

This time around, we were a little more realistic in terms of the timeline. When you do things at a very accelerated pace, costs run up. That's acceptable in a crisis but not otherwise. So we did things more sensibly this time but we did not go back to our old ways. So what we did during the Maggi launch in ten days, we now did, maybe, in fifteen days. But we definitely did not allow anyone to slip back to the four weeks they used to take previously.

Some things have changed. We now let younger people take more decisions and that's always a hard thing to implement in established companies. I can't say that I'll let a junior manager do something and then constantly watch over his or her shoulder. I need to build in the capability to absorb the risk of some mistakes because a junior person will make mistakes as he or she takes on a greater responsibility. But the advantage is that young people can take more risks, they can work harder and faster. And as we move into new areas like marketing on social media and retailing online, young people understand the new technology and channels better.

So is this setting a new normal in the company? Are we now faster than before? Is the pace institutionalized?

Let me put it this way. It's a start. But I will be fooling myself if I said that this has become the new norm. People are talking about the changes; they are seeing the first results in the market. My guess is it will take a few more months, maybe a year or even more for the full effect of what we did to play out through the company and the market. If employees like what they see, if the market recognizes our effort, then people will realize that they were part of something significant and will accept the need to change. That will dissolve the resistance that inevitably crops up when you push change through a hierarchy. Today, a senior guy may impede a junior guy because he thinks someone is being brash. Tomorrow, as the culture changes, that senior guy will not want to seen as an impediment.

The crisis also helped teams to get more proximate. I'm working with Amit Narain in HR to use this opportunity to seed a culture change in the company, to try and embed changes more systematically. If my leadership team and I can do this and if we can create a new normal, then we will have used the crisis well to become an even better organization.

SAP Labs India

SAP Labs India is SAP's largest research and development center outside its headquarters in Germany and is part of a connected network of eighteen Labs. SAP SE (FY15 revenue US$22.8 billion) is a market leader in enterprise application software.

Founded in 1998, SAP Labs India is responsible for SAP core solutions and provides product localization and India-specific solutions. Through a network of three offices in India at Bengaluru, Gurgaon and Pune, and an employee base of over 6,500, SAP Labs India contributes significantly to SAP products such as SAP HANA, a platform for applications and analytics; SAP S/4 HANA, a business applications suite; and several individual applications and solutions.

As a global services and support organization, SAP Labs India has the largest production team outside Germany providing assembly, validation, and test services and accounting for nearly 50 per cent of SAP custom development. In addition, SAP Labs India provides remote maintenance services to approximately 80 per cent of North American customers.

SAP Labs India is noted for its people policies and practices. Great Place to Work has ranked SAP Labs as No. 7 among the best companies to work for in India across all categories, and No. 2 in the information-technology industry.

Dilipkumar Khandelwal (born 1976), the managing director of SAP Labs India and executive vice president, enterprise cloud services, SAP SE, holds a bachelor's degree in engineering from the University of Mumbai and has attended management programs at the Indian School of Business and INSEAD. Equally passionate about technology and business, he seems to typify the restless entrepreneurial culture he wants to foster in the organization.

Leader speak: Dilipkumar Khandelwal

As a development center for SAP, we contribute significantly to the product portfolio in many ways. In the recent past, we have conceptualized and driven solutions such as SAP Fashion Management, SAP Commercial Project Management, SAP Overall Equipment Effectiveness Management, and Visual Manufacturing Planner, among others.

There are two aspects of working at SAP Labs that are powerful facilitators for innovation. One, as a professional you can change your role to pursue an interest. I'm a good example. I started in consulting and have spent time in quality, partner and ecosystems, customer acquisition, presales, development, support, and now in cloud delivery, infrastructure, and key enterprise services. The only thing we ask for is that employees stay in a role at least for two years to add value in that role.

Second, you can change the status quo. A lot of people feel that big companies are rigid. Of course we have processes and they are important because companies need to run efficiently. But those processes are not set in stone, but are constantly checked and adapted.

The best way to describe the freedom at work we have built into the system is that you can be an entrepreneur here. If you have an idea that you think can add value, and if you have the conviction to champion that idea and pursue it vigorously, you will find the company is not just open to change but has structures and initiatives in place to help you develop and run with your idea.

A lot of this stems from our design thinking methodology. If a software development team wants to introduce new features in a product, they have to get their proposed changes vetted by end-users who will use the software. This creates a dialogue among the stakeholders, as different interest groups debate and refine the proposed changes till they reach a consensus. Once you have that consensus, the team is empowered to make the changes.

Design thinking is not restricted to product development; it cuts across everything we do. If you work here, you can challenge the status quo. And if you can come up with a better way of doing something, whether it is food delivery in the cafeteria or software development, you will be empowered to change the process if you can build a consensus. That's what we mean by being entrepreneurial.

We enable change and innovation in many ways. At a basic level, we work closely with the best universities and management institutes so that our developers can benefit from their expertise. We also have put in place processes to stay aware of and work with the vibrant startup culture here in India. This is important because while we are a 44 year old company with our own way of doing things, technology changes outside are so rapid these days that a small startup can easily disrupt established business models. Mobile internet, cloud computing, social media, and other technologies are powerful agents of change and anyone with a new idea can use them to create big ripples.

The SAP Startup Studio, an accelerator program that we started in June 2016, is one of the ways in which we have institutionalized this interaction with startups. Through this initiative, we provide mentoring, infrastructure, and technology support to seed early-stage startup companies. The program is run out of a 75 seat facility at our Bengaluru campus and we incubate startups in select technologies and verticals for a period of one year. Beyond the first year, we provide a strongly knit mentorship program. The program includes guidance and support in building a startup business through access to SAP's huge ecosystem of customers and partners. In addition, startups benefit from access to SAP knowledge experts, venture capitalists, technology visionaries, and academia. SAP and its partner experts will share and mentor the selected startups on emerging trends and technologies. If required, SAP will also take an equity position and refer the startup to SAP's mergers and acquisition team for the next stage of growth. Our first batch of seven startups joined the incubator in 2016.

In addition to working with external startups, we also run a full scale *intrapreneurship* program within SAP which creates a unique opportunity for our employees to explore, develop, and foster new business and technology opportunities to grow and drive organic innovation. This program allows employees to present an idea and a business plan to management. Successful pitches receive internal funding within the working umbrella of SAP.

In addition, we encourage disruptive ideas from employees through our internal SAP Blue program, an enterprise crowdsourcing platform that helps to connect an idea owner (sponsor) with skilled developers (crowd) to take an idea to the next level of maturity. Any sponsor can post an idea on the platform and request colleagues with specific skill sets to apply and work on it. Since the start of SAP Blue in August 2015, we've had more than sixty projects running on the platform and over twenty have been completed. Several projects have resulted in product extensions or new security standards for our portfolio of enterprise software products or have been incorporated into our portfolio of internal productivity applications. The range of projects extends from product development to process development to tool development to process improvement. The program has been so effective that SAP Labs in Brazil, France, US, and China are using it as a template to start innovation platforms in their locations.

Though SAP Blue is primarily intended for internal use, two of the projects have gone external. In one case, a software program developed to analyse big data is being used by a major IPL (Indian Premier League) cricket team to decide the best playing eleven based on the opponent team, pitch conditions, previous history, and so on. In the second case, an app to help visual and hearing impaired individuals in indoor navigation was born out of an Internet of Things project and this app was subsequently unveiled at the India Inclusion Summit 2015.

If your entrepreneurial urge is so strong that you feel you need to explore it independently, our Entrepreneurship Sabbatical policy allows you to take leave of absence from the company and work on your startup for up to two years. If you succeed, we hope you will be our ambassador to the external entrepreneur world. If things don't work out, we will welcome you back so that you can share your learning with us. We introduced this policy in July 2016 and two people have availed of it already.

This is what we mean when we say we are entrepreneurial. We are trying to build a company that is agile, flexible, incorporates change, and brings an idea to development and to the market quickly, either as part of the SAP product portfolio or outside it.

People always ask, what is innovation? To me, innovation is creativity plus monetization. So at a business level, there are delivery commitments that all of us have and these are non-negotiable. But many of us want to do something over and above what is required to meet a business commitment. That's the nature of a development team. People are passionate about learning new things, about doing something new. We try to build the freedom to facilitate that urge.

For instance, we have over eighteen interest groups here in SAP Labs and we fund them all. If you have an interest in music or trekking or drama, you can be reasonably sure of getting a few like-minded people and some resources to pursue that interest. We routinely have external achievers come and talk to us on a wide variety of topics and these different perspectives help us grow. Guest speakers include a former president, eminent authors, film makers, actors, athletes, business leaders, astronauts, journalists, and many others.

People also ask, how do you measure the effectiveness of such initiatives? Beyond a limit, it is futile to even try. In fact, I think we can actually fool ourselves with metrics. Many of our initiatives are designed to help a person to learn, to come out of their comfort zone, to go and do things they haven't done before, and to open up their minds. If they are able to take this back to their work, I believe it creates value.

Putting a metric to such initiatives is difficult. We do monitor the ideas bubbling through the system to see how they are performing. Some of them make it into our products, some of them go to the external world, many fizzle out. We monitor all of this but don't necessarily measure it for the metrics. Ideas that get incorporated into our product portfolio are fairly straightforward to track. But if an external idea, say a startup, succeeds, it becomes harder to quantify the contribution since many different things contribute to a startup's success. So I would be perfectly satisfied if a startup goes out and tells the world that SAP created an impact by helping with the technology, or the skills, or the ecosystem we provided.

At a company level of course, the India team will be evaluated on how much we contribute to the development and support of the global SAP product portfolio. I believe the best way to do that in a software product company in a fast changing technology environment is to build an entrepreneurial culture that has the attitude and the processes in place to embrace and incorporate disruption on an ongoing and daily basis.

Larsen &Toubro

Larsen &Toubro Ltd (FY16 revenue Rs 102,631 crore, US$ 16 billion) is one of India's largest multinational companies with offerings that span technology, engineering, construction, manufacturing, and financial services. The seven-decade old company has customers in over thirty countries, manufacturing facilities in nine countries, including India, and offers design-to-deliver capabilities in the hydrocarbon, infrastructure, power, process industries, and defence sectors.

A M Naik (born 1942), chairman of the L&T group, joined the company in 1965 and rose to become CEO and managing director in 1999, and chairman and managing director in 2003. Naik is an assertive man who revels in his small town roots, and can be alternately overbearing and disarming. *The Economist* once described him as 'a bear of a man. His staff speak of him with awe and tea boys get jumpy near him. And just when you've concluded that Mr Naik is a despot, or has overdosed on propaganda, he will say something devastatingly self-critical.'

When I met Naik, one option was to talk about engineering innovation and capability at L&T. But that is already well documented on the company's website and in their publicly available annual reviews. That was when Deepak Morada, the head of brand strategy and communications, suggested that Naik could perhaps talk about how L&T foiled a takeover by the Birlas in the early 2000s and future-proofed the company against hostile takeovers. It is an unusual example of financial innovation from an engineering company.

On paper, the transaction is simple to describe. In 2001 Grasim Industries, an Aditya Birla group company, acquired 10.45 per cent stake in L&T. The Birlas, who had a competing cement business of their own, were interested in L&T's large cement business. Grasim continued buying L&T shares in the open market, and when their stake crossed 15 per cent, they made an open offer for an additional 20 per cent in line with the acquisition guidelines of the Securities and Exchange Board of India. L&T, under Naik, fought tooth and nail to prevent the Birla takeover. In 2003, after more than a year of negotiations, the Birlas exited L&T by selling their stake to a trust run by L&T employees. In return, the Birlas received L&T's cement division and named it UltraTech.

In reality, the transaction was anything but easy, and involved tense negotiations and intense corporate and political lobbying. The details of this tumultuous David-versus-Goliath corporate saga have never been made public. This is Naik's story.

Leader speak: A M Naik

If you look at our offerings, you will see that we are in more than eighty businesses largely centered on engineering and infrastructure. Whether it is the first, the longest, tallest, heaviest, largest—L&T has done it.

Over the past several decades, we have built the expertise and the track record to make the most of the immense opportunities that India offers today. People have often told me that it can sometimes seem as if almost all the new airports, roads, and power plants are being built by L&T. We have repeatedly set benchmarks, only to surpass them ourselves.

Since 2000, we have developed and rigorously implemented a five-year strategic planning process. We are now in the fourth wave of this program. Our goal is to achieve revenues of two trillion rupees (US$ 30 billion) by 2021 and we intend to do that by narrowing our focus to key areas. These include IT, technology services, infrastructure, defence, smart world, and water management. But none of this would have been possible if we had not survived as a company.

L&T has long been coveted for takeover by different groups. In the late 1980s, the Chabrias tried to take over the company. The L&T management at that time tried to protect the company by inviting the Ambanis to buy a significant stake in the company.

This turned out to be a mixed blessing. While it staved off the threat from the Chabrias, the Ambanis were more interested in L&T's rich cash flow to grow their other businesses. Throughout the 1990s, L&T meandered along without strategic direction.

In late 2001, the Ambanis sold their 10.5 per cent stake in L&T to Grasim Industries owned by Kumar Mangalam Birla's Aditya Birla group. Grasim was a direct competitor to L&T in the cement business and wanted to take over the company.

By this time, I was the CEO and managing director and was in a position to do something about this. It was clear to me that the Birlas were mainly interested in our cement business, and that was just one-third of L&T. But to get the cement business, they wanted to take over the whole company. And since they had no interest in the rest of our business, it was likely that the core engineering business—the heart of L&T would have been sold off. That would have been the end of L&T as we knew it.

I knew it would not be easy to challenge the attempted takeover. I was a simple village boy who had risen on merit in a professionally-managed company. I had no connections to and no experience of working with bureaucrats, politicians, and ministers—the sort of people who matter in corporate takeovers.

On the other side of the equation were the Birlas with four generations of wealth and influence behind them. Remember, they are no ordinary business family. The Birlas have a long history behind them; even Gandhiji used to stay in Birla Kutir in Delhi. That was the kind of clout I would be up against.

What gave me some hope was that there were some people in the government who understood that what L&T did was of strategic importance to the country. They realized that because we operated in several key sectors, it was important that we remain independent. In fact, this was why the government had a 32 per cent stake in L&T held through various financial institutions. It was meant to safeguard L&T against takeovers.

Two influential people, who had worked with a major media house and who realized the importance of L&T remaining independent, set up a meeting for me with a very senior cabinet minister so that I could make my case.

It turned out to be a strange meeting. Here I was making a case for how L&T was of strategic importance to the country and should therefore be allowed to remain independent. But all that the politician knew about L&T was that we made world-class roads! Nothing much came out of that meeting.

It was then that I realized how much work had to be done to educate and persuade the influencers and decision makers. I became a regular visitor to Delhi meeting the political leadership to project the critical role played by L&T in strategic sectors of India's economy.

For a long time, I did not make any headway. My efforts were seen by some government officials as non-cooperative. I remember one government official, who represented the government shareholding, once telling me that I was creating boardroom standoffs because I would not agree to sell out. I replied saying that all I wanted was a fair valuation of the cement business. The standoff continued.

Then, in a cabinet reshuffle some key portfolios changed, and some of the new ministers understood the merits of L&T's case and vigorously championed our cause. They prevailed on the then prime minister not to support any takeover of L&T.

All this took place over several months and many meetings. After months of negotiations, a person close to the Birlas but someone who also understood why L&T should remain independent, offered to mediate.

We all agreed that the Birlas would exit with L&T's cement business and in return, they would sell their entire stake of L&T shares, worth 425 crore rupees, to the L&T Employees Welfare Foundation, a trust run by employees.

Now we had to generate the funds for the Employees Foundation to buy Birlas' stake. To enable this, the government allowed L&T to extend an interest-free loan of 275 crore rupees to the Foundation, repayable in 11 years. The remaining 150 crore rupees was borrowed from two banks.

To service the loan, L&T employees were encouraged to contribute to the Employees Foundation. In exchange, we gave them a seven-year debenture with a promise to repay the money with a five per cent post-tax return. This brought in 110 crore rupees into the kitty. Of this, we used 25 crore to repay the first installment of the 275-crore-rupee loan taken from L&T, and used the rest to start repaying the bank loans. We repaid one bank within a year.

Simultaneously, this was in 2003, the economy started improving and with it our business started growing faster. That resulted in a healthy dividend income and we used this dividend money to repay the loan from the second bank.

As the business continued to improve, our dividends kept increasing steadily. It went up from 40 crore rupees a year all the way to 100 crore rupees in subsequent years. This helped us to repay our loans much faster than expected. We repaid the employee loans in four years instead of seven years, and repaid the L&T loan in eight years instead of eleven years.

So the L&T Employees Welfare Foundation today owns 12.3 per cent of L&T stock that we effectively bought without spending a single rupee in net cost. Everything was paid out of dividends earned in the business. I can't think of a better example of financial innovation.

Incidentally, that 12.3 per cent stake, which was bought for 425 crore rupees is now worth more than 15,000 crore rupees. This is L&T's biggest insurance against any future hostile takeover bid.

But how did we get here? What caused this massive rise in valuation?

In 2002, at the time of the open offer by the Birlas to acquire 20 per cent stake, the paid up equity share capital of L&T was just 250 crore rupees.

After several rounds of negotiations, we agreed to split the equity with 25 crore rupees remaining with L&T and 225 crore rupees going to Birla. That was because all our assets were mainly associated with the cement and shipping businesses, and cement was being demerged to Birla. The rest of our business, the core engineering business, was asset-light.

And since the Birlas were taking over the assets of the cement business, they also took over the associated debt. The removal of the cement related debt had an instant effect on L&T's balance sheet. Because of the debt incurred for the cement business, L&T had an over-leveraged balance sheet with a debt-to-equity ratio of 1.1 to 1. As a result, our CRISIL rating had been downgraded from AAA to AA+.

The moment the debt from the cement business was removed from our books, our debt-to-equity ratio improved to 0.19 to 1. Overnight, our CRISIL rating reverted to AAA and our EVA (economic value added) improved from minus 350 crore rupees to plus 50 crore rupees, a positive swing of 400 crore rupees.

The last part of this exercise was valuation. The government appointed ICRA, a rating service, to value the company, and they arrived at a valuation of 291 rupees per L&T share. It was left to L&T and the Birlas to negotiate the split in valuation between the cement business and the rest of the business for the demerger.

After several rounds of negotiations, we agreed to split the valuation as 120 rupees per share for all of L&T's non-cement businesses, and 171 rupees per share for the cement business.

And since L&T had issued shares to employees at an average price of 178 rupees per share, the board deducted 171 rupees as the price of the cement business from the share price to arrive at an L&T share price of seven rupees per share (on a face value of one rupee).

And that was it. The saga was over. In the end, both L&T and the Birlas achieved their goals. Both of us continue to do business with each other on many fronts.

So what did we achieve? One, L&T got out of the non-core cement business. When I became the CEO, I had publicly stated that L&T would get out of cement because our core business was engineering, and cement was a distraction that consumed disproportionate capital. But I was determined to sell the cement business only at a fair price. We achieved that.

Two, we lightened our balance sheet and improved our credit rating from AA+ to AAA.

Three, we improved our economic value add (EVA) from minus 350 crore rupees to plus 50 crore rupees.

Fourteen years have passed since the demerger. How have we fared since then?

The L&T share, worth seven rupees at the time of the cement demerger, is now worth 11,000 rupees if you account for the many splits and bonuses since then.

Thousands of our employees have become millionaires and billionaires. I don't know what they intend to do with their money but I can tell you what I have done with mine.

I come from a middle-class background and I never expected to be wealthy. So I have used the money from my shares to build schools and hospitals and other institutions in Gujarat, my *janmabhumi* (land of birth), and plan to build a modern hospital in Mumbai, my *karmabhumi* (place of work).

To me, this is what all innovation should result in. It is not about how clever you are. What matters is what you do for others given your ability and circumstances.

HDFC Bank

HDFC Bank was set up in 1994 and is now India's second largest and most successful private bank. In FY16, it reported revenue of Rs 70,973 crore ($10.9 billion), total assets of 708,846 crore rupees($109 billion), net interest margin of 4.3 per cent, and has the highest stock market capitalization among all Indian banks, public or private.

HDFC Bank's business is split almost equally between retail and corporate banking and it is making a strong push into digital and rural banking to expand its reach and network. The bank's performance is all the more creditable considering that the banking sector in India has been underperforming for several quarters due to tepid credit growth and significant non-performing assets.

'As far as banking is concerned, demand for financial services exceeds supply, so market is not an issue. And it is unlikely to be an issue for the next ten to fifteen years,' says Aditya Puri (born 1950), the managing director of HDFC Bank. Puri, a former Citibanker, was appointed in September 1994 and is the longest serving head of any bank in the country.

When HDFC Bank started in the mid nineties, 80 per cent of the market was with the public-sector banks. They had the distribution and the largely metro-centric private banks had the better products and technology. So Puri and his team figured that if they could combine distribution, brand, and product in a market where demand exceeds supply, they 'should have more than a reasonable chance of succeeding.'

The founding team also realized that the world was changing rapidly. Technology, telecom, and media were exploding and so people would be far more aware of what was happening in the world and would demand more from their banks. So the benchmarks for HDFC Bank would need to be pegged to what was world-class and not just to what was good in India.

The first thing the founding team did was to identify and recruit the right people for building such a bank. And so they hired people from many world-class organizations, namely, Bank of America, Citibank, UBS, Arthur Andersen, Reserve Bank of India, and Pricewaterhouse.

Then they defined their target market. *What products should they bring to the market? What kind of technology would serve them both in the present and in the future?* And most of all, *what should be the culture and the brand value of the organization?*

The bank was clear they wanted to straddle the country's GDP (gross domestic product) and wanted to service the entire C + I + G spectrum (consumption, investment, and government spending). This meant that the target market would span corporate, retail, wholesale, and small-scale banking, and the bank would need a fair amount of geographic diversification.

On the technology front, the bank took a call and opted for centralized processing and distributed servicing based on open systems. This meant they could add capacity as needed without being boxed in to a mainframe computing architecture.

And finally, the founding team said they would price appropriately taking risk and reward into account so that the bank could survive for the long run.

As far as ethics were concerned, the bank had the benefit of having the reputed HDFC brand behind them. The bank wanted to be a place where people enjoyed working and they wanted to be a brand that stands for integrity, customer convenience, and trust. These tenets could not be violated either in terms of regulations or in giving the wrong product to the customer.

Once HFCC Bank opened shop, it grew rapidly. 'Since we came up with cutting-edge products and because we had the technology, we were using cutting-edge telecommunications to provide information as well as products to the customer, and we grew pretty rapidly,' says Puri.

In fact, the initial concern was how to service the demand and live up to the brand promise. So they started by serving the large corporate houses, which, as a class, had the lowest risk but was the most difficult to penetrate in terms of competition. Then they went to the smaller corporates and simultaneously started retail banking. This was the story for first five to seven years.

That was when Puri and his team figured that digital technology would become big in banking and that would enable them to go to the semi-urban and rural market where 60 per cent of India lives. That market was totally underserved but could not be reached through the conventional branch banking business model.

The bank figured it would need three or four years to create an appropriate business model and that would also be when enabling technology and mobile access devices would allow them to use machine intelligence.

The technology came together around 2010 by which time the bank was ready with an appropriate set of products and services. HDFC Bank tested the semi urban and rural markets and then scaled up. 'With digital a lot of things changed,' says Puri. 'Digital allowed you to access lot of information. It allowed you to have access to customers through multiple devices. It allowed you to reduce your cost by using shared networks through cloud computing. It allowed you to have straight through processing.'

Going digital also protected the bank from the threat of disruption from the new startups mushrooming in the financial services space. HDFC Bank figured that the startups were not talking about changing the banking system; instead they were piggy backing on it. They were building products and services that sit on top of the technology platforms that banks had painstakingly and expensively built over the years.

The bank decided not to let that happen to them. They asked themselves, 'What prevents us from doing what these startups are doing?' 'Why shouldn't we disrupt ourselves?'

The first HDFC Bank branch, opened in 1995, was backed by a core banking system offering real-time banking for the first time in India. In 2000, the bank became an early adopter of data warehousing and analytics in the country. That focus on technology has carried over to the bank's push into digital banking to extend reach and increase responsiveness.

The HDFC Bank website is now a virtual branch open 24×7. Powered with search, select, and buy features, the site receives over thirteen million visitors a month, making it one of the most visited financial services sites in the country.

The NetBanking service offers over 175 online transactions and real-time processing allowing the bank to offer financial benefits to customers instantly. For example, deposits start earning interest instantly, and mutual fund orders get the benefit of same day pricing.

The MobileBanking service offers over seventy-five transactions across all smart-phone platforms. Customers can click-to-call or use online forms to get loans, open an account, or get access to the closest bank branch or ATM.

The bank uses analytics to track consumer behaviour and build richer customer profiles, gauge needs, and make targeted offerings through their preferred channel be it a branch, ATM, mobile, net banking, or email. Existing customers with adequate credit scores are offered instant credit cards and *10 second loans*.

The PayZapp digital wallet is a complete and secure payment system that enables customers to search, compare, shop, transfer money, recharge mobile phones and data cards.

The Wholesale Banking solutions enable business to business collections, payments, and supply chain trading processes to be done online or through mobiles.

The Kisan Gold Card portfolio of solutions and apps helps rural customers to apply for loans, extend existing ones, and provides information on *mandi* (market) prices and government schemes. KGC Tez offers agricultural loans within three to four days, KGC Turant enables eligible farmers to enhance their loans or credit in just a few seconds by sending a text message or through an ATM, and the Kisan Dhan Shakti account helps farmers through convenient cash-flow based repayment schedules.

The WatchBanking solution takes this convenience a step ahead into wearable technology. The bank is experimenting with robotics and blockchain to see how it can best apply these new technologies to repetitive sequential transactions. To make the online experience secure, the bank works with in-house and third-party experts to monitor and shut down phishing and Trojan infested sites.

Can HDFC Bank keep up the pace? How will it continue to adapt to change?

The bank's approach is to deliberately embrace disruption and incorporate it into their portfolio of products and services. So if you were a customer and interested in operating a digital wallet or shopping online, you don't need to go outside the bank's system and share your financial information with anyone else. The bank offers you that convenience through its own online, offline, and mobile channels.

As for keeping abreast of change, Puri says that speed is baked into the bank's culture. He points out that the bank has been changing every three or four years. It began as a bank that mainly served large corporate customers. Now, in addition, they are a retail bank, a bank to small and medium businesses, a bank to rural customers, and a bank to people at the bottom of the pyramid. The bank has been changing its technology, upgrading the platform as needed, adding new products, and changing their access devices to stay current. As illustration of this pace, Puri says the bank implemented its digital initiative in just six months

But the technology is not intrusive. If a customer who is uncomfortable with technology wants to deposit cash, staff at a branch will help him do it. But they will also show him how it can be done in a simple way through an ATM or through net banking or mobile banking. In time, that customer may be comfortable making the change to digital if he sees value in the convenience and control over the transaction when using digital channels.

Enabling this convenience at the back end is not difficult, says Puri. Yes, the bank needs to add expertise in digital technology, marketing, analytics, and related technologies. But that is a small team of maybe 200 or 300 people in a workforce of 80,000.

'If you keep your eye on the customers and see what they want, and if you deliver it to them with your brand values, you'll be all right,' says Puri, 'but customer needs change every six months and you need to have the flexibility to cope with that.'

Infosys

For many years, Infosys was the poster boy of the Indian IT services revolution. Started in 1981 by N R Narayana Murthy and six others, the company spent the first decade in obscurity. After the economic reforms of 1991, when it became easier to move people and technology across borders, Infosys developed its global delivery model of software development using a combination of onsite work at client locations in the west and offshore software development in India.

This was the start of the golden period for Infosys. The milestones went flashing by as a juggernaut was born and gathered pace. In 1993, Infosys went public and introduced an employee stock option plan that went on to create some of India's first salaried millionaires. The company crossed $100 million in revenue in 1999 and was listed on the Nasdaq stock exchange in the US—the first Indian company to do so. Revenues crossed $500 million in 2002, $1 billion in 2004, and $2 billion in 2006. It had taken Infosys twenty-three years to reach its first billion in revenue and just twenty-three months to reach its second billion. This was also the year when Narayana Murthy retired from the company on turning sixty. He continued as chairman.

Infosys continued to grow, crossing $5 billion in revenues in 2010 and ended FY16 with revenue of $9.5 billion. But as software outsourcing slowed due to the economic slowdown and political backlash from the west and as machine intelligence and automation eliminated the need for labour-intensive programming, the Indian IT industry, including Infosys, was seen in need for a reboot. In 2014, Infosys appointed its first non-promoter CEO, an outsider from SAP, and is now reinventing itself.

N R Narayana Murthy (born 1946), the founder and chairman of Infosys, holds a master's degree in computer science from the Indian Institute of Technology Kanpur, and is widely acknowledged to have led two path-breaking innovations. One, he pioneered the global delivery model of software development. Two, he raised the level of disclosure and transparency in financial reporting and created a benchmark that others had to follow or be left behind.

In his autobiography, S Ramadorai, a former CEO and vice chairman of TCS, India's largest IT services company and an Infosys competitor, asserts that TCS, and not Infosys, pioneered the offshore outsourcing concept. He says Infosys just marketed itself better. Sandeep Dhingra, previously a financial analyst with Jardine Fleming who tracked the Indian IT industry in its heyday in the 2000s, acknowledges that TCS has a longer history. 'But until it went public in 2004, TCS was an opaque company,' says Dhingra, now a fund manager in Singapore. 'Infosys used good corporate disclosures and listing in the US to build a strong brand not just for itself but also for the Indian IT industry. We must remember that the banks and financial institutions are the biggest spenders in IT, and being a well known and highly regarded entity in the financial markets is a great marketing advantage.'

Many industry watchers admiringly speak about the company's core-versus-context branding strategy to differentiate itself. They say Infosys realized early on that at its core, most Indian IT services companies were similar; they offered smart and inexpensive programming talent to western clients. But Infosys realized that Fortune 500 companies in the west were wary of outsourcing work to India because India was seen as a remote sweatshop with dodgy corporate governance. So Infosys created campus-like offices with food courts and playgrounds that attracted top talent, reported its financials in internationally accepted formats, listed on Indian and US stock exchanges, and provided a compelling context for companies to engage with it.

Leader speak: N R Narayana Murthy

When Infosys started in the eighties, the regulatory environment in India was very anti-business. So we decided that if we had to succeed, we had to formalize a model that leveraged the power of globalization. I defined globalization as sourcing capital from where it is cheapest; sourcing talent from where it is the best available;, producing from where it is most cost-effective; and selling where the markets are, without being constrained by national boundaries.

We decided to leverage this power of globalization by creating a software factory in India.This required us to select good people, to take them through high quality training, to provide them good physical infrastructure, to provide them good technological infrastructure, to put in place processes that enhanced quality and productivity that compressed cycle time, and execute as high a percentage of the work as possible from scalable, talent-rich, process-driven and cost-competitive countries like India. This, we thought, would provide value to our customers and create differentiation. Infosys was the first company to do all of this. That was our competitive advantage.

We had started developing software from India as early as 1984; but doing it on a factory scale started only from 1992 after the economic liberalization. Liberalization abolished licensing. It provided current account convertibility that helped us to start offices abroad, eased overseas travel, and allowed us to hire experts from abroad in areas such as quality, productivity, branding, and so on. So I would say our growth, the actualization of our strategy and dream started in 1992.

Now of course the global development model has become the industry standard. But we pioneered it.

Our differentiation was two-fold: one, in creating a formal business model based on globalization, and two, in recruiting high quality talent and taking them through rigorous training.

Even today, no company has training like we had at Infosys. We take people through eight months of training. We have the world's largest training facility; nobody else in the world has anything like this. We are the first company to get certified to CMM Level 4 and CMM Level 5, Malcolm Baldrige, and many other benchmarks. We spend probably the highest percentage of revenue on technology among all similar companies.

When you recruit good-quality people, when you take them through good training, when you provide them good technologies and good infrastructure and good processes, then you are bound to provide value to your customers. That was our differentiation.

The transparency that we came to be known for was an extension of this same approach. We realized that excellence in any organization has to be all-pervasive. You cannot say that I will produce excellent software but that my offices can be dirty. You cannot say that I will produce excellent software but our financial reporting can be questionable. An organization that aims to embrace excellence has to embrace it in every dimension.

That is why we said we will get listed on an Indian stock exchange first and then get listed on a US stock exchange. We said we will advance good governance practices in India. So we were the first company in India that introduced quarterly reporting on a voluntary basis; now it has become standard, it has become mandatory. We were the first ones to fully comply with the Cadbury Report; no other Indian company had done that. We are the first Indian company to be listed on the Nasdaq; we were one of the top ten companies on the Nasdaq to fully comply with Sarbanes-Oxley Act of 2002. We were the first Indian company, and one of the very few in the world, that gave away as much as 35 per cent of our equity to our employees—at current prices that is approximately fourteen billion dollars. Nobody in India has done that, not even one-tenth of it. For us it was just being excellent in every dimension. For us it has to be organic; it has to be all pervasive.

People say we were good at marketing ourselves. But this was not a marketing exercise; it was just the way of running a good company. We felt that if you raise the trust of your customers by not short-changing them, by delivering what you promised on time, within budget, with the requisite quality, if you are transparent with your investors and follow the finest principles of corporate governance, if you treat your fellow employees with respect and dignity and share wealth with them, if you treat your vendor partners fairly, if you don't violate any law of the land, if you create goodwill in the society, then we felt that the rest of it would follow. Profits, market cap, all of it would follow if we stayed true to our vision.

Building such a company was not difficult because that is the way we have been brought up. This is what our parents taught us; this is what our teachers taught us. We did not do this as an exercise to become more attractive to anybody. We said this is the way we will run our business. You cannot run away from your values just because you are now in business.

People ask me, 'Isn't this a very personalized way of running a company? What happens when the founders leave? How do you institutionalize what you believe in?'

You can institutionalize vision if you recruit people who are smarter than you and have values that align with yours, provide them with a nurturing environment, and hope that they will carry on what you started.

There is no guarantee that it will work. But then, there is no guarantee for many other things in business. There is no guarantee that you will grow, no guarantee that you will continue your quality initiative, no guarantee that you will bring in innovation, no guarantee that you will be financially transparent.

But there are a couple of things you can do as a leader to better the odds of succeeding.

First, lead by example. If I demonstrate that I arrive in office on time, that I use my time effectively, that I go into details and ask deep questions, then my team would want to emulate me and their teams would want to emulate them. The only way you can help youngsters appreciate the value of what you say is when your actions speak louder than your words.

Second, hire the right people. If you want people to build a good company that lasts, you have to select competent people. Do they have the capacity to learn quickly? Do they have character? It's not easy finding the right people but you need to spend the time and effort to do this well. Having found the right people, you have to train them. If they are convinced, and if they have a passion for what you are saying, they will use that learning to grow the organization and themselves. There is no other way.

Many people have asked me why we spent so much money on training at Infosys. No other software company does that, they said. Not in India, not anywhere in the world. We did it for a simple reason. If we want to serve our customers well, we have to train our people well. In our business, technology changes rapidly. We go from country to country; we go from applications to applications. The only constant for us is change. So training is the only way by which we can enable our people to serve our customers better.

Everything that you do as a leader—communicating a vision, providing a nurturing environment, training and mentoring, behaving in a fair and transparent manner, creating and sharing wealth, and instilling values through personal example— ultimately leads to trust.

If people trust you, they will accept huge sacrifices. Trust is important because following a vision means a long journey, lots of sacrifices, and deferred gratification. If you want thousands of people to commit to your vision, if you want to build a company that lasts for decades, you have to build trust.

After all, that was how people walked with Moses. Yes, the sea parted. But there was no guarantee that it would.

Tata Motors: Commercial Vehicles

Tata Motors (FY16 revenue Rs 276,542 crore, US$42.5 billion) is India's largest automobile company. The company has three main lines of business: Jaguar Land Rover, a UK-based high-end vehicle business acquired from Ford in 2008; the commercial vehicles business; and a passenger cars business.

The commercial vehicle business is organized under two categories, M&HCV (medium and heavy commercial vehicles) and LCV (light commercial vehicles), and covers a wide range of products, including trucks from sub one-tonne capacity to forty-nine-tonne mass movers, and passenger transporters from five-seater mini vans to sixty-five-seater buses.

The M&HCV segment, where Tata Motors is among the top five manufacturers globally, includes trucks, tractors, buses, tippers, and multi-axle vehicles with gross vehicle weight (vehicle weight plus payload) from 7.5 tonne to 49 tonne. This includes the Prima range of heavy duty trucks and a range of buses ranging from intercity coaches to school buses to ambulances.

The LCV range covers pickup trucks and small commercial vehicles. This includes the Tata Ace series, India's first indigenously developed mini-truck with a sub one-tonne capacity, the Magic passenger variant developed on the Tata Ace platform, and the Winger. The company also offers the Cityride and Starbus range of buses in the LCV segment.

Tata Motors is the dominant player in the commercial vehicles segment in India but its market share has slid from a near monopoly when it started in the fifties to 68 per cent in FY10 to

46 per cent in FY16. There is competition both in the LCV segment from established players such as Mahindra & Mahindra, and in the M&HCV segment from new players such as Bharat Benz, part of German auto major Daimler.

Ravi Pisharody (born 1955), the executive director in charge of commercial vehicles at Tata Motors and an alumnus of the Indian Institute of Technology, Kharagpur and the Indian Institute of Management, Calcutta, is the man in the middle of the truck wars. In the eighties, Tata Motors successfully fended off Japanese competition in the LCV segment with its indigenously developed Tata 407 light truck that went on to become a runaway success. Pisharody and his team hope to repeat that story as they innovate to stay ahead of a resurgent competition.

Leader speak: Ravi Pisharody

Tata Motors is perhaps the only commercial vehicle manufacturer anywhere with a product portfolio that spans everything from a mini truck costing 250 thousand rupees to a seven-million rupee truck to a twenty-million rupee hybrid diesel-electric bus. This is unique in the industry and it presents unique challenges as every market segment requires to be nurtured individually. Historically, we've been fairly good at doing this. Since starting the commercial vehicle business in the 1950s, Tata Motors has routinely created new market segments, be it in pickup trucks and small commercial vehicles, or recently the Tata Ace mini truck and Magic passenger vehicles based on the Ace platform.

In the bus segment, the convention was that the manufactures would build the chassis and customers—whether private operators or state-owned transport corporations—would build the bodies. Since the bodies were often not of high quality, they reduced the productivity and longevity of the bus. So in the early 2000s we decided to deliver completely-built buses, a segment first in India. We do this with our joint venture with Marcopolo, a leading Brazilian bus body manufacturer, and also manufacture fully-built buses through our partner, Automobile Corporation of Goa Ltd.

Change is a slow process in the commercial vehicle business. Unlike passenger cars that are bought for convenience or pleasure, commercial vehicles are bought for business. Truck owners are primarily interested in keeping costs down.

Every country has its own operating cycle. The operating cycle in Germany with high-speed driving on the autobahns is very different from that in India where it is common to have significant overloads, lower speeds, and frequent stops at check posts.

In the five years or so that a commercial vehicle owner in India retains his vehicle before selling it, the typical annual operating cost is split somewhat like this: 50 per cent towards fuel, 15 to 20 per cent towards tyres; and 10 to 15 per cent towards repaying the loan taken to buy the vehicle. So a lot of our innovation is focused on improving fuel economy since that is the biggest cost for a truck owner.

One example of this would be the lift axle that we designed and introduced in India. Around 2005, trucks had migrated from the typical two-axle chassis to three-axle and multi-axle chassis. We designed the third axle so that it could be lifted off the ground. This is useful when a truck makes a trip with a full load requiring all wheels on the ground but makes the return trip with a lighter load or with no load. In that case, the third axle can be lifted to save wear and tear on the tyres attached to them. This not only prolongs tyre life but also improves fuel economy because of lower friction. Lift axle trucks are now common in India but we introduced them in the country and enjoyed an early mover advantage for three to four years.

Another innovation we introduced to improve fuel economy was radial tyres for trucks. While radial tyres in cars have been around for a long time, radial tyres in trucks in India are an innovation that we introduced as recently as 2007.

Radial tyres cost more than conventional tyres but our analysis showed that over the life of the vehicle, the savings from the increased fuel economy would quickly offset and surpass the incremental cost of their initial purchase. The challenge was to convince truck owners about this since the incremental cost of radial tyres is not insignificant considering that a truck can have anywhere from four to ten tyres.

In fact, even tyre manufacturers were reluctant to make radial tyres for trucks since there was no demand for them. So, we initially imported radial tyres even at the risk of annoying our tyre suppliers and demonstrated over a period of three or four years that the savings from the improved fuel economy more than offset the rise in initial tyre cost. The industry has now more or less moved to radial tyres and Indian tyre manufactures have developed capacity to make them.

Our goal is to reduce the total operating cost to a truck owner by five to seven per cent every year. This can only happen through continuous innovation. It could be through a new design such as the lift axle, a new product specification such as a radial tyre, or even an incremental improvement in the drive train so than an engine oil change can be deferred for a longer interval. Every little helps considering that a truck runs about 200,000 kilometres a year.

In products that we have developed on our own, like the Tata Ace, our innovations are home grown since these products are designed ground up for Indian conditions. But even when we don't have our own product in a segment of interest to us, we catch up quickly. The best example of the latter would be the LCV segment where we did not have a product in the eighties when the market saw the entry of a slew of products by Japanese companies such as Mitsubishi, Mazda, Nissan and others. Tata Motors came back strongly with a four-tonne truck called the 407 and that model has become so successful that it is now virtually a brand by itself in the LCV segment.

Innovation in the trucks business goes well beyond product design. The channel is a critical factor. Some of our distributors have been with us for decades and they are now run by the second and third generation in their families. These relationships are difficult to replicate and become a differentiator for us. Unlike a car that tends to be driven in and around its place of purchase, a truck travels the length and breadth of the country. So dealerships and service centres play a critical role in delivering a consistent user-experience to long-distance drivers and truck owners. We try to have a Tata service centre every fifty kilometres or so. These centres have a common look and feel and have the same rate card for labour and spare parts. So a trucker in Delhi can get his vehicle serviced in Chennai for almost the same price, even accounting for the marginal difference in local taxes.

The competitive landscape is changing. In the early 2000s, there were just four to five players in the commercial vehicle space in India. That has now increased with global giants such as Daimler and Volvo already in India and others considering to set up shop.

The reason for this interest in India is due to a combination of factors. Our roads are improving. Tax reforms, such as the goods and services tax, hold out the promise of reducing frequent stops for check posts at state borders. Tightening emission standards are bringing India closer to international standards. All this means that the technology in the trucks on Indian roads will improve and this makes India attractive for global players who have historically been unable to adapt their portfolio of vehicles to India, traditionally a low-tech and low-cost truck market.

Tata Motors is ready for the coming changes. The government has declared its intention to move to BS-4 emission standards by April 2017 and to BS-6 in 2020. This is a huge challenge. All our trucks up to 16 tonnes use our own engines and we have been doing a lot of work to make them ready for the new standards. For trucks of 16 tonnes and above, we work through our sister company Tata Cummins, a joint venture with Cummins of USA, to develop engines that are emission-compliant and suited to Indian conditions.

Also, as our overseas revenues have grown (20 per cent of our revenue now comes from outside India), we are no longer designing and building our products purely for the Indian environment. For example, the benchmark for our Tata Prima series of heavy duty long-distance trucks are the best-in-class European trucks from makers like Daimler, Man, and others. Prima was launched in 2009 and growth in that segment has been slow because it is ahead of its time. That's because while these large trucks can slash travel time for a full load by 40 to 50 per cent and result in significant gains for an operator, these savings can only be realized if the trucks can run for long spells without interruption on good roads with few or no check posts. That is not the case in India now. But as we move toward better roads and reduced stops, this segment will become important.

Similarly, in the medium and light segment we have invested in a brand called Ultra which is benchmarked against the global Japanese leaders and are expected to do very well in more developed markets such as South Africa and Thailand.

To improve our global footprint, we have built assembly units in Nigeria and Tunisia and are starting one in Kenya. We have a manufacturing unit in South Africa. We now export to Asia-Pacific markets in Thailand, Philippines, Vietnam, Indonesia, and Malaysia, right up to Australia, and to the South American markets of Chile, Venezuela, and Bolivia.

We are also ramping up our bus business. In 2016, the company won orders for around 5,000 buses from different state transport units across the country and some of these buses will use advanced technology. For example, we are building hybrid buses for Mumbai, and articulated buses for Karnataka that will have a second car trailing the main one. The bus market is still small in India and this is also a reflection of the state of our public transport. For every five trucks sold in India we probably sell one bus. In China, where infrastructure and public transport is better, that ratio is more like two buses sold for every three trucks sold. As and when our infrastructure improves, we will be ready to supply the demand.

Asian Paints

Asian Paints Ltd (FY16 revenue Rs 15,534 crore, $2.4 billion) is India's largest and Asia's second-largest paint company. Started in 1942, the company operates in 19 countries and has 26 manufacturing facilities worldwide servicing consumers in over 65 countries. Asian Paints has a long history of using customer insights and technology to innovate and stay ahead. Their 53 per cent market share in India is more than that of the next two competitors combined.

KBS Anand (born 1955), the managing director, CEO, and an alumnus of the Indian Institute of Technology, Bombay, and the Indian Institute of Management, Calcutta, is an affable man with an easy efficiency about him. My interview is a good example. I sent a meeting request through Twitter, his office responded on email, and the meeting was scheduled without even a phone call. It was that unfussy and straightforward.

Leader speak: KBS Anand

When we started in the 1940s, paint was largely imported and sold through big-city wholesalers. Nobody wanted to stock an Indian brand. So our founders were forced to go to the small towns and found themselves talking to the actual person who sells paint to the consumer. They learned that the European shades were not the ones that consumers wanted. Consumers wanted the dark aquamarines and the deep oranges and they wanted them for unexpected uses, for example, to paint the horns of cattle during the Pongal festival in Tamil Nadu, or the Pola festival in Maharastra. And they wanted paint in small quantities.

We became the only company supplying such paints and that created a demand in the rural markets. But obviously you can't cater to every dealer directly. So when other shops also wanted our products, they came to the wholesaler in Mumbai and asked for Asian Paints. That created a reverse pressure and demand for our products grew.

I don't think anybody consciously sat down and said, 'let's be innovative'. It was just that we had our backs to the wall because the established channels wouldn't sell our paints and so we went out and created a market for ourselves.

It was the same backs-to-the-wall pressure that spurred what is now considered to be another big innovation we initiated back then.

Painting used to be a very Diwali-centric activity in those days and most paint companies would give dealers six months to one year of credit. So in most cases, you collected money for what you had sold last Diwali.

As a small company with no money— I'm talking about the late 50s and early 60s—Asian Paints couldn't afford such long payment cycles. So we went to the dealers and said, 'If you pay regularly within 45 days, we will give you an additional discount at the end of the year. But you must pay every bill within 45 days. And if you pay in cash in advance, we will add an extra five per cent discount.'

Even today, 70 per cent of our sales are on advance payment. As a result, our working capital is much lower than many other companies. Now of course, every other paint company also does this and it has become the industry norm. Maybe they need to add another fifteen to thirty days credit because they have to compete with us. I don't think this kind of advance payments works in the paint industry anywhere else in the world.

In a way, the paint industry is in what I call a lucky category. Like everyone else, we too are affected by the slowdown and our growth rates have dropped from 15 per cent volume growth till a few years back to the low double-digits now. It's not an ideal situation but it's better than a lot of other industries.

The reason we are growing is because the number of households is constantly going up, disposable incomes have gone up, and the cost of paint as a fraction of the painting cost is going down.

All over the country, joint families are being replaced by nuclear families and disposable incomes are rising as women increasingly join the workforce. All over the country, urbanization is increasing. In fact, states like Punjab and Kerala are just one large urban sprawl. So the sheer number of houses to paint is rising exponentially and people increasingly have the money to get them painted.

The second thing that has happened is that the cost of labour has shot up. Labour cost used to 15 per cent of the cost of painting earlier; it is now about 60 per cent. So it doesn't make any sense to use *chuna* (limestone) or other low-cost alternatives to paint your house now, when, for a slightly higher price, you can go for better paint. We see this premiumization across our all categories—among our three or four qualities of emulsion paints, the most expensive category is growing the fastest. The premium paint may be 20 per cent costlier than the base version but the impact on the total cost of painting is less than 10 per cent.

Positioning innovation

One thing that we have consciously done over the last several years is to change the perception of paint from a maintenance product to a décor product. This was triggered by something that I saw during one of our consumer focus group exercises in Bengaluru about fifteen years ago. During the course of the exercise, a participant in a focus group made a surprising statement. He said he repainted his house every Diwali. Conventional wisdom then was that the painting cycle was maybe three years or five years.

There was a reason he painted his house every Diwali—well, it turned out that he actually painted only his living room. It made his family feel good. He said it was the cheapest way to feel good and celebrate Diwali.

That insight to consumer behavior was a revelation to me. It ties in with the many other social changes that have taken place in recent years. The younger generation today spends more. While their parents may have saved all their lives and bought a house after retirement, they buy homes within five years of starting work. They live on credit because they are confident that tomorrow is going to be better than today. Add to this mix increasing women empowerment and nuclear families and we now have a situation where people are prepared to spend significant amounts of money to feel good, and women have a major say in those spending decisions.

Product innovation

These insights into consumer behaviour have been translated into our products in many ways. So a lot of what we do in our paints these days—to provide faux finishes, effects, color combinations, and recently even wallpaper—are ways to help a consumer, and particularly the lady of the house, to change the look of a house, to freshen it up, to feel good.

The other insight we had was that customers will pay for convenience. We were the first paint company anywhere to start a home painting service. It helps us draw in customers who would otherwise not consider us. For example, I once met customer who used this service. He runs a nursing clinic in Kolkata and he was painting his house after fifteen years. Money clearly wasn't the issue so I asked him what kept him from painting his house all these years. It turned out that he was so put off by the thought of buying paint, hiring painters, supervising the project, and getting the house cleaned at the end that he kept delaying the decision. For him, our painting service was a boon. We still don't paint very many homes because the cost of our service is a little higher than the local painter because we have to factor in additional costs such as employee benefits and so on. But for some people, the convenience is worth the slight premium.

Retail innovation

One of our biggest innovations in recent years is our line of Signature stores. We have three of them currently: a 6500 square feet store in Bandra, Mumbai, another one in Connaught Place, New Delhi, and a smaller one in Kolkata. The Signature stores don't sell paint. They offer visitors an immersive and fun experience about painting their home. You can chose among different colors and finishes, visualize how your rooms will look after painting, experiment endlessly, and get expert advice from our consultants. If, at the end of the experience, you'd like buy our paint or get your house painted by us, we are happy to do that too!

Even with no advertising, these Signature stores get roughly eighty visitors a day and they spend close to an hour there. The stores have been massively influential in building brand awareness.

We spent a bomb on these Signature stores and so there is a limit on how many we can build. But we have replicated parts of these stores in dealer locations across the country. These properties are called Colour Ideas and are portions of a store ranging from three hundred to one thousand square feet where we offer a truncated version of the Signature store experience. We now have over three hundred of them across the country and they are a big hit with consumers.

An associated idea that has worked very well for us is colour consultancy. Currently available in about twenty-two cities, this is a service where a colour consultant can visit customers at home with advice on colours, products, finishes, and so on. Last year we recorded more than 260,000 such visits.

Technology innovation

Asian Paints has always used technology as a differentiator. We were one of the first companies in India to buy a mainframe. Not one of the first paint companies, one of the first companies per se. This was in the early seventies and we used it not for accounting but for forecasting and distribution of paint. By that point I think we had twenty-three depots or so, and thousands of SKUs (stock keeping unit). Keeping track of what was going to sell, where, and when, was a nightmare. The branch manager used to place an order with the factory which would then produce to fulfill the order and dispatch it. This would inevitably result in a longer time to deliver. So everybody built a buffer and that added cost.

What the forecasting system did was to predict fortnightly demand of each SKU across each depot in the country. It worked brilliantly. The forecasting software was developed internally and it ran on the mainframe. Remember, this was the time when you had to program computers using cards and the process was complex.

Later on, we were equally proactive in moving to the personal computer age at which time all our branches were linked and our accounting was computerized. We moved to packaged software like SAP only in the early 2000s; till then most of our software was developed in-house.

Communication innovation

Paint as a category doesn't really interest consumers. It's one of those things you apply to a wall and most of the time you don't even care whose product you have used. So building a consumer brand is not easy in this category. You can build a brand with a shopkeeper or the applicator but building a brand with a consumer is tough.

So what we did was to use emotion to build a link with the customer in our advertising and communication. In the 90s our advertising was centred on festivals and marriages since that was when India painted its homes. Festivals are a celebration and painting a home was part of the celebration.

That has changed. Now India paints all the time. Now painting is about décor, about feeling good. In fact, many people avoid painting at Diwali because it's difficult to get painters. Instead, people look at painting when it's convenient, for example when the kids don't have examinations, and so on. So painting goes on pretty much throughout the year.

Around 2000 or so, we did quite a lot of research to understand consumer behavior. Up until then, we relied on the FMCG (fast moving consumer goods) approach to marketing where individual products are branded. But what we found was that the consumer only knew one brand, Asian Paints. They had no clue or interest about all the different product names we were promoting. So we changed our entire branding approach and changed the focus from the product to the consumer.

It was based on this research that we ran a very popular advertising campaign called *Har ghar kuch kehta hai, ki iske andar kaun rehta hai*. Every house tells a story of the people who live in it. What the research showed was that for the consumer the most important things is his life were his family and his home. And paint is one thing that adds value to the home or can help create a home of the person's choice.

Information is plentiful, insight is rare

I don't want to give the impression that all our innovations and ideas worked. For example, our Colour Ideas store took final shape after maybe seven or eight trials of what would work in a paint shop.

A lot of ideas fail because they are born out of your understanding of the consumer; the consumer may actually be different from your perception of him or her. This is because consumers vary across categories and the categories evolve and change. There is the double-income category that is internet savvy; they like lots of information, will visit your experience stores, and welcome colour consultants. Then there are the new rich who want the latest and fanciest finishes; they will come and literally ask the shopkeeper about what is the latest. Then there is the government employee and the retired segment; they look for value.

But of course people don't fit neatly into such pat categories. Segments overlap and even within segments, people don't behave the same. So you have to be aware that even when deriving insight from market research, that insight is not perfect. Sometimes it may even lead you astray; for example, everybody talks about going green but except perhaps for asthmatic consumers, no one will pay a rupee more for green paint. So you have to take research with a pinch of salt. Interpreting research is tougher than the research.

Dr Reddy's Laboratories

Dr. Reddy's Laboratories Ltd (FY16 revenue Rs 15,471 crore, $2.4 billion) is one of India's largest pharmaceutical companies. Founded in 1984 by Dr K Anji Reddy, the company manufactures over 200 medications which are sold across the world. The company employs over 20,000 people and has twenty manufacturing facilities and ten R&D centres worldwide.

Through its three businesses, pharmaceutical services and active ingredients, global generics, and proprietary products, Dr. Reddy's offers a portfolio of products and services including APIs (Active Pharmaceutical Ingredients), custom pharmaceutical services, generics, biosimilars, and differentiated formulations. The company's therapeutic areas of focus are gastro-intestinal, cardiovascular, diabetology, oncology, pain management, and dermatology. Dr. Reddy's major markets include USA, India, Russia and CIS, and Europe.

Dr Reddy's is one of the few Indian pharmaceutical companies to have actively pursued new drug discovery and development. The company started new drug discovery research in 1993 but, after lackluster results, has now spun off drug discovery to Aurigene, a Bengaluru-based and independently-funded subsidiary. Aurigene out-licenses molecules that have reached some stage of development to pharmaceutical companies globally for onward development. This defrays the cost of research and generates revenue through milestone payments as the molecule journeys through the drug development process.

GV Prasad (born 1960), the co-chairman and CEO of Dr Reddy's Laboratories, holds a bachelor's degree in chemical engineering from the Illinois Institute of Technology and a master's degree in industrial administration from Purdue University. Prasad, along with brother-in-law and chairman Satish Reddy, has transformed the company from its research-led legacy to a more patient-centric business.

Leader speak: G V Prasad

We started in the eighties by making APIs (Active Pharmaceutical Ingredient, the active component in a drug) for global and US customers who in turn were formulating and selling them as generic drugs. We felt this was something we could do ourselves. When a drug comes off patent in the US, generic drug manufactures can file an ANDA (Abbreviated New Drug Application) to make and market a generic equivalent. Generic drugs are far cheaper than patented drugs and have a large market.

We felt that with our lower costs of manufacturing and better backward integration, we had a good chance of succeeding in the US generics market on our own. In those days, only one other Indian company was attempting this in the US.

We were initially apprehensive about the acceptance of an Indian company in the US. But it turned out that once a product is approved by the US FDA (Food and Drug Administration), the buyer doesn't care where it comes from.

Our first win was Fluoxetine, a generic antidepressant drug and a replacement for Prozac. From then on, we went from strength to strength. We set up a plant in Bachupally in Telengana at an investment of forty crore rupees which was a big bet for us considering that our revenue at that time was about 200 crore rupees. But the initiative paid off, and by early 2000s we had expanded into emerging markets in addition to the US. Today we sell more than 200 medications around the world.

I think the reason we succeeded is that we have an entrepreneurial mindset. We were never worried about challenging patents and submitting ANDA applications. We went after the opportunities with the best talent and domain expertise we could hire. We invested both in manufacturing at the back end, and in sales and marketing at the front end. In the process we built the skills needed to go after the generics opportunity, and that was how we added value and differentiated ourselves from the competition.

When Dr Reddy's started, the focus was on discovering new drug molecules. The founder, Dr Anji Reddy, was a scientist and that focus was natural for him. But the cost of discovering a new molecule and taking it from concept to market through clinical trials is now estimated at about $2.5 billion. Very few companies can afford that risk. We are clear that we cannot afford it.

So in 2009, we moved our drug discovery initiative to an independently-funded subsidiary. This subsidiary, Aurigene, works by collaborating with large global pharmaceutical companies and out-licensing our molecules when they reach a certain stage in research and development. This conserves our investment and has the potential to generate revenue through milestone-based payments as the molecule is developed further by those companies by way of research, pre-clinical and clinical trials and so on.

As for Dr Reddy's, we've changed our focus from being a science-first company to a patient-first company. This means that instead of looking for new molecules to discover, we now look at the disease first. We look at the patient first. *What does the market need? Is that market viable?* So for example, if diabetes is a well-served market, we are not likely to enter it because there is little value we can add in such a well-served market.

So we now look for niches, for white space in the treatment gaps. And we work backwards from those opportunities. What products should be design for an opportunity? What would be a good delivery method? What are the animal and human clinical trials we should consider?

This is a quasi new product-development approach to drug discovery and lessens risk. We are increasing the odds of success because we are now meeting an unmet need in the market. This is incremental innovation.

Our recent innovation, ZEMBRACE SymTouch injection, a drug-device combination product intended for acute migraine sufferers is an example of this approach. As anyone suffering from migraine knows, you can feel the onset of a migraine episode but a pill does not work fast enough to treat it. Our product is intended for self use by a patient and is injected subcutaneously and acts rapidly. The product was approved by the FDA in early 2016 and is our first branded product in neurology.

We are now extending this product for delivery as a nasal spray. A nasal spray is an alternative to people who do not like the thought of injecting themselves; since it is ingested through the membrane, a nasal spray is almost as quick acting as an injectible. We are working on more such examples of incremental innovation in other areas, for example, in dermatology.

The idea is to start from the disease and work backwards to create either a drug variant or a delivery variant. We call this reverse translation. The process still requires all the rigor of clinical trials but is far more limited in scope than new drug discovery. Compared to the $2 million to $5 million that it typically costs to develop a generic drug, a reverse translation drug costs anywhere between $20 million to $40 million to develop. This is a significant sum of money but it is a lot lesser than the billion and more dollars needed for new drug discovery. So even if we will no longer bet the company on discovering a completely new drug, we will continue to pursue the reverse translation type of research to participate in parts of the novel drug value chain.

We also innovate in other ways. For example, combining drugs is an opportunity. This is commonplace in India but is not as common in some of our other markets. An example of such a combination would be to create drugs that lessen the load on patients taking multiple drugs. This is especially helpful for elderly patients who take several medications at a time. Even if you have a family member or a care giver looking after you, and this is rare in many countries now, it becomes almost impossible to monitor the medicine count and dosage for multiple medications. Combination drugs help by combining one or more medications and reducing the medication load.

The change in mindset in moving from being a molecule-centric company to a patient-centric company has changed our approach to the business in a fundamental way. Previously, we would be elated on developing and marketing an API or a generic. Today, we are doing much more to understand the needs of the patient. We use a design-thinking approach to understand a patient's journey to health and we are using the insights from such exercises to create services, modify the product and packaging, and making the experience more patient-friendly. It's a different way of looking at the business. We are in the early stages of this journey and we are learning as we go. What it means is having much deeper interactions with patients and hospitals, hackathons to generate innovation in products and services, and setting up of a design studio to simulate real-world conditions all along the delivery chain. The patient, and not the drug, is now the focus of our business.

The Indian pharmaceutical industry is frequently in the news for coming under the US FDA radar. The reason why this happens is mostly due to culture. The US has a transparent regulatory environment and FDA regulations, while tough, are not that difficult to follow. The problem arises because of our fondness for *jugaad* or quick fixes. This is the same mentality that makes us cut across a lawn even though there is a path around it and a sign that says, 'Don't walk on the grass'. That mentality of bypassing established procedures is what gets us into trouble in a highly regulated and quality-conscious environment.

In our own case, the challenge has been to establish processes so that quality becomes ingrained in the culture of the company. This is a function of both scale and culture. In the initial days, when we were not so big, I would visit and inspect our factories frequently. That kind of close supervision from senior management ensured strict compliance to processes and ensured a high level of quality. As we grow, the challenge is to institutionalize processes so that quality and compliance to processes are not compromised across multiple layers of supervision. It's a problem common to all companies. The big global companies like GE or Toyota or Bayer or Pfizer have perfected the process over decades. We'll also get there in time.

One of the ways in which we are addressing this problem is through a programme called SMT (self managed teams). Under this programme, we hire people who have completed high school. Over the next few years, these graduates are put through a combination of academic coursework and rotation through various departments in the company. Depending on their choices and aptitude, they go on earn diplomas or degrees in science, engineering, and management. Over 2,500 people have been through the programme and they have progressed in a variety of roles in the organization from plant operators to quality personnel to scientists to managers. The SMT program not only helps us to give back to society but also allows us to build a core of operational people steeped in our quality and culture. It is a game changer and we are very excited about the programme. You see kids who are barely out of school or college and now they are doing recipe management on the computer. It sets the bar high for everyone else in the company.

The other thing that we need to do as an industry to improve quality is to reduce our reliance on contract labour. In highly regulated industries like pharmaceuticals, it bothers me that companies hire contract staff for production line work. Such workers do not have the same training and culture sensitization as regular staff. And they are paid lower wages. To expect lower-paid and lesser-trained contract workers to perform to the same high standards as a full time employee is unreasonable and it should come as no surprise that this can lead to negative surprises during FDA and other quality and safety related inspections. At Dr Reddy's we do not use contract staff on our production lines. In fact, we try to avoid it everywhere. If people are required for unskilled tasks such as housekeeping, we use service contracts and outsource such work. If you aspire for excellence, as we do, you cannot say that I'll be excellent in R&D but I'll compromise in other areas to cut costs. You have to maintain high standards all over.

Titan

Titan Company Ltd (FY16 revenue Rs 11,278 crore, $1.7 billion) is a joint venture between the Tata group and Tamil Nadu Industrial Development Corporation. The company was set up in 1984 and has four lines of business: watches and accessories; jewellery; eyewear; and precision engineering. Many of its brands—Titan watches, Tanishq jewellery, Fastrack accessories, and Skinn perfumes—are household names.

Titan positions itself as a sophisticated but not elitist alternative in all its categories. When it started, the public-sector company HMT ruled the wrist watch market with robust mechanical watches. Titan brought in quartz watches that had an international look and feel and yet retained a distinctly Indian identity. Its iconic Edge series of wrist watches, launched in 2002 and promoted as the 'thinnest watch in the universe', fired the public imagination. It was a remarkable recovery for a company that had—buoyed by its early success in India—overreached in the nineties by expanding too much and too fast in Europe and nearly gone bankrupt.

Tanishq, the jewellery brand started in 1995, had a rocky start. It started with eighteen-carat gold and diamond jewellery in international designs sold through up-market stores and found no traction. It now offers a more comprehensive collection with a more pronounced Indian sensibility. A Tanishq innovation, the Karatmeter, a non-destructive way to test the purity of gold, has been hugely successful in promoting the company's image as a seller of genuine gold. Fastrack was launched in 1998 as an irreverent urban youth brand of accessories.

Bhaskar Bhat (born 1954), managing director of Titan, is an alumnus of the Indian Institute of Technology, Madras and Indian

Institute of Management, Ahmedabad, and has been with the company since 1988. An excellent raconteur, Bhat recounts with wry humour how innovation throughout Titan's history has often resulted from not focusing unduly on market research.

Leader speak: Bhaskar Bhat

Throughout our history, we've taken many decisions that have been subsequently described by others as innovative and disruptive. At the time we took those decisions, they seemed to us to be a logical choice based on our reading of the situation. But as a company we also have an impulsive and restless gene in our DNA and when I look back on some of our major inflection points, these have been the result of this curious combination of logical thinking and impulsiveness.

Let's start with our entry into the watch market. In the eighties, 99 per cent of the watches in India were mechanical watches. The only quartz watches most people had then seen were cheap digital watches that looked terrible, went bad quickly, were not water resistant, and could not be repaired because there were no spares or service outlets. And since the market leader, HMT, was a public-sector company with a ponderous sales and service setup, conventional market research would have told us to become a more friendly alternative to the existing product.

We read the market differently. Xerxes Desai and J R D Tata, the people who started Titan, felt that the market was in fact, ready to change to something new. So Titan entered the market with analogue quartz watches. Our watches were beautifully designed, they were built to high quality, and they were sold in sales and service outlets that looked modern and friendly. The watches were a great hit and in time they wiped out mechanical watches in India.

We were hailed as great disrupters. But for us, this was just a logical reading of the market. We felt that quartz watches were the future because they were accurate, didn't need winding, could be designed better because they could be made slimmer; and because they had lesser moving parts, quartz watches could be made cheaper. Yes, making a good quartz watch meant bringing in world-class technology and manufacturing in India, but if we at Tata could not do that, *who* could? That was the logic. The impulsiveness was that we really didn't rely on any great market research to validate the proposition. We jumped right in and the rest is history.

Our foray into jewellery with Tanishq is another example of this curious combination of using logic and impulsiveness to arrive at big decisions.

The jewellery market in the mid nineties was highly unorganized and dominated by the family jeweller. There was no guarantee on the purity of the gold and customers were being routinely cheated. The only large-format stores were few and far in between, say TBZ in Mumbai, GRT in Chennai, and a handful of others elsewhere. And people would say that they were buying jewellery as an investment, as a store of wealth.

We thought this situation was ripe for change. When we looked at the census data of 1981 and 1991, we saw a changing profile of women in urban India. There were now more educated, they were beginning to aspire to greater freedom, and more and more of them were in well-paying jobs as the IT industry took root and the economy threw up new opportunities. To us, it seemed logical that such a woman would buy jewellery for adornment and not for investment. She'd buy jewellery to look good, not just to save for the future. And since women were now far more mobile than before, the stranglehold of the family jeweller would loosen and eventually disappear.

All this seemed logical to us.

But conventional market research would have dictated that the best way to address such an opportunity would be to mimic the TBZs and the GRTs and become an alternate to the trusted family jeweller.

That's where the impulsiveness comes in. We took a different route. We thought the emerging Indian urban woman would welcome something completely different from what was then available in the market. So we set up a national chain of branded outlets to sell diamond jewellery set in eighteen carat gold that looked international in both design and quality. We guaranteed the purity of our stones and gold. And our Tanishq stores reflected this look with their up-market and international ambience. Our logic was that this was a strategy that had worked for us in watches. With our mastery in manufacturing and experience in retailing high-quality branded merchandise at a national level, we thought we could not go wrong.

The experiment bombed initially. We ended up with a very alluring brand but women said, this is not for me. India at that time—this was in 1994—was very much a twenty-two carat gold country. In retrospect, we were ahead of our time because now tastes have changed and people are much more ready to try new things.

But we stayed the course and made corrections. Our basic premise didn't change. We said, surely jewellers can't cheat customers forever. Surely, a woman deserves better design than what is available in all those other stores. We believed that if women were now buying branded watches and branded apparel, why wouldn't they buy branded jewellery? It was only a matter of time.

So we expanded our portfolio to include both traditional and international designs, and we offered twenty-two carat gold in addition to eighteen carat used to set diamonds. Once we got our product mix right, the customers came.

Our learning was that we needed to position ourselves appropriately. We are a sophisticated brand but not an elitist one. We appeal to the midmarket segment. Yes, we want to be a little different and stand out and be known for our class and style, but we do not want to stray too far from what a middleclass or an upper middleclass urban woman thinks is elegant and stylish. So we create a *Tanishqization* of her view of what jewellery should be like. We push the envelope on design, but not to a point where our customer is uncomfortable with what she sees.

Simultaneously, we introduced the Karatmeter, a simple non-destructive way to test the purity of gold in all our stores. You can bring any piece of jewellery to our stores and place it inside the machine and in 180 seconds, you will know its purity.

This was a revolutionary act when we introduced it and there were, and continue to be, lots of instances where people have discovered that the jewellery they bought or were gifted were of lower than promised purity. We've had in-laws quarreling in our shops and we've had direct conflicts with the trade but the fact is that a lot of what is sold as twenty-two carat gold in India is twenty carats or below.

So what Tanishq did, apart from bringing guaranteed pure jewellery with high-quality manufacturing and design to women across India, is that it moved the industry to a higher standard.

Customers are now much more aware and demand better products and quality across the market.

The reason we were able to scale the jewellery business to the national level is because of another innovation, this time on the production side. At our plant in Hosur in Tamil Nadu, we have what is called Karigar Park to house artisans from all over India. Normally goldsmiths and artisans work in cramped, and unhygienic shops in by-lanes of gold streets across India. They suffer from toxic fumes, work long hours for low pay, and lead a difficult life. At Karigar Park, we house them in quarters, provide them an air-conditioned factory work environment, and pay good wages. It makes perfect business sense for us because their productivity is now high and we get the best of traditional designs, in addition to our international designs, at scale.

Though our curious combination of logical thinking and impulsive action has been good for us as a company, there was one instance where it went horribly wrong and that became the trigger for a fundamental change in the way we work.

This happed in the mid nineties. We were having great success with Titan quartz watches and buoyed by that success, we decided to expand into Europe using the same strategy that had worked so well for us in India.

Our belief was that European customers, like customers in India, would appreciate good design and manufacturing. The thinking was that we had a great design team and manufacturing facilities in India and if we could supplement that with some design inputs from Europe, we could deliver well-designed and high-quality products to European customers. After all, Titan was a world-class watch with Swiss machinery, Japanese case manufacturing facility, French movement, and Indian costs.

So we set up retail outlets across Europe in several countries including the UK, Spain, Portugal, Greece, and Austria. We worked with creative agencies and design teams in Europe to make our product relevant to those markets. We used local marketing and advertising agencies to communicate our value proposition. We really had a great product and it was marketed well.

We failed spectacularly. Sales never picked up and through the nineties, we kept ratcheting up the losses. In the early 2000s, we accepted the reality and closed down our European foray at a dead loss.

Looking back after so many years, I really can't see what we could have done better. If I had to pick any one reason for why we failed, it would be that we could not overcome the country-of-origin barrier. Unlike the USA, Europe is still fairly insular. Most European customers still prefer to buy European brands, be it a car or watch or anything else. They just could not accept that a well designed world-class watch could come out of India.

That experience was a wakeup call for the company. When we went to the Tata group for funds to bail us out after the crisis, they bluntly told us to earn the right to grow.

Till then, we were a company that reveled in our passion and creativity. We realized that we now had to combine that with much better business acumen because at the end of the day, this was a business and shareholders needed to see revenue and growth.

When I took over from Xerxes Desai, I was clear that I wanted to retain the passion and creativity that was his hallmark. But I also wanted to inculcate processes and accountability.

It is difficult to put a name to this curious mix of logic and passion we have now encoded in the company but if I had to put a label to it, I would say that in our DNA there is something that I would call collective dreaming.

Let me explain. If you were to talk to our brand managers and marketing people in a formalized setting, they would probably sound like anyone else in the FMCG or retail industry and you would hear about market research and data and so on.

But put these people in a room where we are discussing a new product line or design or strategy and you would see passionate advocacy and strong points of view. This is our DNA, this logic plus passion, and we've tried to institutionalize it over the years.

It starts with transparency. As a company, we communicate extensively with all our stakeholders— with our customers, employees, associates, dealers, the trade, everyone.

As a customer, you can not only get clear and detailed information about our products and pricing, you can also go to our website and see videos of the actual factory where our *Karigars* work to produce the jewellery you buy.

Transparency leads to trust. We tell our people everything, good news and bad news. They know when the business is good and we share the success in tangible ways. They also know when the business is bad and so when we ask them to support us through tough times, they know it is for genuine reasons.

We've built on this transparency and trust to create ownership. At our yearly strategy planning events, we get people into a room and ask them to dream about where the company should be in a year or five years. These are not soft exercises. We ask them to pin down goals and articulate a path to achieve those goals. We ask them to boil it down to elevator pitches and ask them to take ownership of those goals. And we encourage the owners to use a consultative approach to reaching their goals. This means that if someone promises to bring in a result by a certain date, it is that person's responsibility to sell that project down the line to bring it to fruition. That requires passion and commitment.

And once a year, we randomly survey employees across levels in the company to see how effective these exercises are: *did we achieve what we set out to do?* Or, *do they feel the company is on the right track?* And so on. It is a process that has been perfected over several years and the objective is to balance our collective dreaming with execution excellence. Many new initiatives have come of this process including the Fastrack youth brand, GoldPlus, the mass-market Eyewear brand, and the scaling up of our precision engineering business.

Since our manufacturing facility is in Hosur, we tend to hear a lot of Tamil on the shop floor and is in the corridors. I realized how much the culture had changed when people only half-jokingly said that previously they could hear the CEO say words like '*enada, vaada, poda*' ('how are you, come, go'). Now instead, they increasingly hear '*Ebitda*'! (a financial acronym for earnings before interest, depreciation, and tax)

We were a 700-crore rupee company when we started this exercise and now we are at about 12,000 crore rupees in revenue. So maybe we are doing a few things right.

Marico

Marico Ltd (FY16 revenue Rs 6132 crore, $940 million) is a Mumbai based consumer product group in the beauty and wellness space. It owns over twenty-five brands in hair care, skin care, edible oils, health foods, male grooming, and fabric care, including household names such as Parachute, Saffola, Hair & Care, Nihar, Livon, Set Wet, Mediker, and Revive.

Harsh C. Mariwala (born 1951), chairman, joined his family-owned firm, Bombay Oil Industries Ltd in 1971 and pushed for its evolution from a commodity trading business to branded offerings. In 1990, Mariwala spun off Marico Ltd from the family business and has since then built a consumer product company that avoids head-on confrontation with the large FMCG multinationals but competes with them vigorously in niche areas. In 2014, Mariwala stepped down as managing director at Marico in favor of a professional CEO but continues to run the skin-care business, Kaya Ltd, as chairman and managing director.

Mariwala brings an unusual personal touch to business. When I contacted his office for a meeting, his assistant asked me to email him directly. He likes to prepare his own schedule, she told me with a touch of amused resignation. True. During our meeting, Mariwala was interrupted by someone calling to schedule an appointment. He excused himself, took the call, and made a note in his diary with an old-fashioned fountain pen.

Leader speak: Harsh Mariwala

When I joined the family business in the early seventies, we had a chemical business, a spice extraction business, and an edible oil business. At that time, we supplied edible oil to industrial users and also sold it loose; it was a commodity business.

I believed we could improve the edible oil business significantly if we changed it to a branded offering. So we branded our coconut oil as Parachute, expanded the distribution chain to interior and rural markets, and quickly grew to a 20 per cent market share at which point we stagnated.

I realized we needed a differentiator to separate us from the competition. I thought one good way to do that would be to change the packaging of the product from tin to plastic. To my mind, plastic was cheaper, more attractive, and easier to store and pour. But when I proposed the idea to our distributors, they flatly turned me down. It turned out that people had tried plastic packaging previously and failed. The bottles had been attacked by rats and they had leaked and so the trade had no interest in repeating the messy experiment.

So we worked with our suppliers to design and build a cylindrical bottle that would stack easily, was not susceptible to rodent bites, and were capped in such a way that it would not spill or leak. It took us nearly three years to convince the trade to stock our plastic bottles and it took us about eight years to move the consumers from tin to plastic. One of our follow-ups to the plastic bottle innovation was a tiny one-rupee mini bottle that helped us counter the sachet revolution. Today we have a 70 per cent market share in branded coconut oil and this is no small part to due to continuous innovation on our packaging.

Another example of product innovation is how we extended our Saffola brand of heart-friendly cooking oil to oats. Oats was a natural brand extension since it is considered a healthy heart food. Our differentiator was to use the insight from our market research that Indians liked their breakfasts to be savoury and not sweet. And since the cereals and oats in the market then were served either in plain or sweet flavors, we created Saffola Oats in mildly spicy and salt flavors. Today, our range of Saffola masala oats is a market leader in that segment.

A similar thing happened when we acquired Mediker, a shampoo brand, from Proctor & Gamble. Mediker was a leader in the niche segment of anti-lice medicated shampoos. But we knew from our oil business that the market for hair oil is far bigger than the market for shampoo. So we developed Mediker in an oil format to complement the existing product portfolio and sales doubled in six months.

Again, it was consumer insight pointing to a real need in the market that led us to launch Kaya Skin Clinics. We opened the first clinic in 2002 and today we have more than 100 clinics across India and the Middle East offering skin and hair care treatments.

So innovation to me is anything that is done differently—that adds value. I call it creating the 'right to win'. You must create a right to win in the market, a competitive differentiator that makes you more compelling to the consumer than the competition. It could be a process. It could be a product. It could be a way of doing things. But it has to add value. And you must continue to earn and sustain your right to win through innovation. Whatever advantage you have initially will be copied by others and so you have to continuously innovate to stay ahead.

Culture is key

In trying to create and add value, you will experiment a lot. You will prototype a lot. You will fail a lot. You have to have the right mindset in the organization to innovate and that mindset comes from the culture you have in the organization.

So it is very important that leaders set the right perspective on why innovation is important. You have to send across the message that every person in the organization can innovate; that innovation is not restricted to a brand manager, a product manager, or an R&D person.

Innovation happens across the organization. It happens through a lot of dialogue when people discuss ideas and trigger a chain of events.

For this to happen, you need to have the right kind of people—people who think differently. You need diversity in talent. You need people who speak out, who will debate ideas and be open to feedback. You need to encourage people to take risks.

You know that old saying, 'You win some, you lose some'? At Marico, we have a different take on it. We say, sometimes you win and sometimes you *learn* rather than losing.

I strongly believe that every failure is an opportunity to learn and make changes. If you start punishing failures, people will stop taking risks. At an organizational level, we try very hard to apply this principle at a practical level. So, for example, if somebody who is up for promotion or a raise or any other advancement takes up an initiative and fails at it, we see to it that the person is not denied that raise or advancement because of it. Otherwise not just the person, but the entire organization will start becoming risk-averse.

Culture is also driven by the values you espouse in an organization. At Marico we strongly believe in openness, trust, and transparency. Without these, you cannot create a culture where people are encouraged to take risks without a fear of failure.

Many times, these value statements remain on paper. What we've done to implement them is to weave them into our policies and practices. To give a couple of examples, we design our offices to facilitate easy access and conversations. We have done away with musters and attendance sheets. Employees do not have to get approvals for routine business expenses. Sick and casual leave do not require prior permission. Little things like that. Of course we have guidelines for what is acceptable and not acceptable behaviour and major violations are punished swiftly. But by and large, when people see that you run an open and transparent organization, they will reciprocate with honesty and goodwill.

To encourage diversity in talent, we recruit people from different backgrounds and put them in a flat organizational structure. While this is empowering, in the sense that you can work across silos without undue hierarchy, it also makes people highly accountable for their actions. So, for example, if you are responsible for driving a brand, you more or less own that activity and so you tend to think more innovatively because you are responsible for your actions. There is not much scope for passing the buck. And these decisions can cover the entire gamut of product attributes from packaging to promotion to pricing or what have you. If you have the culture where everybody thinks differently, then you will have far more innovations.

Execution is critical

It took us three years to convince the Parachute coconut oil distribution channel to move from tins to plastic bottles and it took eight years for consumers to fully accept it. So we learned early on that while you may have an innovative idea, you should never underestimate the effort that is sometimes needed to make others see value in your idea.

Any innovation, and particularly a new product innovation, is a big risk. However much you debate ideas internally, there is no shortcut to actually testing it in the field.

One way to reduce the risk is through prototyping. For example, you can launch a new product in limited geographies or regions, or through selected channels and you use this prototype phase as a laboratory to observe, learn, and make changes. It could be a pricing change. It could be a packaging change. It could be a formulation change. So until you achieve your best option or your standards for rolling it out nationally, you go on prototyping and go on tweaking your product offering to try and arrive at the right mix.

For example, while we test marketed the new Saffola Masala Oats product, we would have experimented with different price points, multiple packaging options, and so on. These tests are important because there are always tradeoffs to be made. A higher price point will allow you to back the product with stronger advertising, for instance. No amount of simulation will give you these insights; you have to test the options in the market.

Leadership matters

The role of leadership in innovation is two-fold. One is to go on demanding innovation. So if I have a presentation from a brand about their next year's plans, they know that I will ask them about what they are planning to do to move the needle on the brand. It could be a new way to market the product, it could be a change in media buying, it could a promotion scheme, or it could be a change in the formulation because research shows it is time to change. Point is, whether it is a small change or a big change, they will be prepared to talk about innovation because I have set the right expectations.

Secondly, top management should reinforce innovation. So if somebody's innovated something that is unique, then you need to make that person a hero or a team that hero. You need to celebrate their success so that others can listen and learn from that experience. So we have innovation awards where we call for entries from everyone from managers to the factory hands and we ask them not only what was the innovation, but how that innovation happened. This is important because then people get to know the process of arriving at an innovation. If you can share the learning and the successes, you can create a buzz around innovation in the organization. People will begin to think about it and work towards it.

Biocon

Biocon Ltd (FY16 revenue Rs 3570 crore, $549 million) is India's largest biopharmaceutical company. The company's business is organized into four verticals:

(1) small molecules comprising a portfolio of APIs (active pharmaceutical ingredient, the main component in a drug) such as statins, immunosuppressants, speciality molecules, and generic formulations,

(2) biologics comprising novel biologics and biosimilars including rh-insulin, insulin analogues, monoclonal antibodies and recombinant proteins,

(3) branded formulations that include 80 plus brands in India and UAE, and

(4) contract research services for overseas and domestic customers.

In contrast to conventional drugs that are synthesized from chemicals, a biologic is manufactured in a living system such as a microorganism or plant or animal cells. Most biologics are large, complex molecules and produced using recombinant DNA technology. They potentially offer the most effective means to treat a variety of medical conditions that presently have no other treatments available. A biosimilar is the biopharmaceutical equivalent of a generic drug and is designed to have active properties similar to one that has previously been licensed.

Today, Biocon's revenue split is approximately 42 per cent from small molecules, 12 per cent from biologics, 14 per cent from branded formulations, and 32 per cent from contract research. In coming years, the company expects a much greater contribution from their biological products as they enter markets across the world after long years spent in R&D.

Kiran Mazumdar Shaw (born 1953), chairman and managing director, started Biocon in 1978 as a joint venture with an Irish company of the same name. A qualified brew master with a master's degree from Ballarat University in Australia, Mazumdar Shaw began by producing industrial enzymes and later expanded into biopharmaceuticals. In 1989, the Irish company was acquired by Unilever who in turn sold it to ICI in 1997. In 1998, Mazumdar Shaw and her husband John Shaw bought out ICI. In 2004, the company went public, the first Indian biotech company to do so. A science-led company, Biocon has continuously innovated since inception in a business noted for its high capital costs and long gestation periods for drug development. Mazumdar Shaw is a forceful speaker and while she has no problem talking about revenue and profit margins, she is at her passionate best when talking about the science that powers her business.

Leader speak: Kiran Mazumdar Shaw

I started Biocon as a biotech company focused on enzyme technologies. I trained as a brew master and so I was very familiar with fermentation technology and enzymes. The first set of enzymes I made was for beer-making because I was familiar with that technology. So whether it was papain to tenderize meat, or cellulolytic enzymes to ferment alcohol and biofuels, or pectinases to make fruit juice, we started producing a range of products. In almost all cases, we started from scratch and developed our own processes and generated a lot of intellectual property in the process. At that time, this was in the eighties and nineties, we had an Irish company as our joint venture partner.

At the time, I was looking for funding to scale up the technology we had developed and was finding it hard to convince anybody to give us money. This was in 1989 and I was looking for a little over one crore rupees. It was not a small sum in those days and no one was prepared to fund us. Remember, in those days funding meant a loan at 15 to 16 per cent interest but even that was considered risky. 'Why do you want to risk money on your own technology?' I was asked. 'Get proven technology from abroad.'

But I was adamant about developing my own technology. I genuinely believed it was superior to what we could get from elsewhere, and in any case, I wanted to own the technology. It was central to our business.

It was then that I met Narayanan Vaghul of ICICI. He helped me get funding through the newly set up TDICI (Technology Development and Information Company of India), one of India's first venture capital funds. To my delight, it was not a loan. Instead, they wanted 20 per cent stake in the company for the money and I was happy to give them that and avoid a loan. So now the company was 30 per cent owned by the Irish partner, 20 per cent owned by TDICI, and 50 per cent owned by me.

When Unilever acquired our Irish partner in 1989 and discovered that we had created so much IP assets, they bought out TDICI's 20 per cent stake within a year for four times the price that TDICI paid—that was the value they saw in the IP. So now Unilever had 50 per cent stake in the enzymes business and they encouraged us to create a portfolio of patents to protect and monetize the IP. So we created patents both in India and abroad.

The business did very well, and with Unilever behind me, we were soon exporting enzymes all over the world.

But in 1998, I decided to pivot from the enzymes business to biopharmaceuticals. We were doing about seventy-five crore rupees in revenues at that time and I figured that sooner or later I would hit a plateau because the enzymes market is not very large.

On the other hand, the pharmaceuticals market was huge and I figured that with the enzyme technologies that we had developed and patented, we could potentially do very well in biopharmaceuticals. We had developed a lot of microbial enzymes and so we started looking at pharmaceuticals made by fermentation. That's how we went in for statins and immunosuppressants; they were produced by fermentation technology.

Then I looked at recombinant technologies that we were using for enzymes. We had developed a pichia fermentation technology, a microbial recombinant technology that we could use to make insulin and insulin analogues. The only thing I didn't have as enzymes was mammalian cell culture technology for antibodies. We hadn't needed that for making enzymes but we needed it for pharmaceuticals. It was not easy to get that technology because nobody would give it to us. After an extensive search, I obtained it from Cuba.

I have never wanted Biocon to be a me-too company. That is why, even today, we are the only company in the world making insulin using pichia technology. We have our own proprietary technology for pichia. Novo Nordisk uses Saccharomyces. Eli Lilly uses E. coli. Sanofi uses E. coli. We use pichia.

There were a lot of sceptics who said that Biocon is using some strange new technology, they will never get regulatory approval. Well, we did get regulatory approval. The advantage of using pichia technology is that it is a very high-yielding strain and it's easy to purify. We developed it initially for producing phytase enzymes and so it was a natural progression for us.

In 2007, we sold the enzyme business. By that time, the pharma business had grown to five times the enzymes business and I knew my interest and future was in pharma. So I sold the enzymes business to our biggest competitor, Novozymes, and they continue to run that business very well from their facility right next to our own facility in Bengaluru. They paid us five times our revenue, which was the value they saw in it. They still use the technologies that we developed.

Since then, the biopharma business has been growing rapidly and we've invested a lot of time and effort on the biologics business. When we talk of biosimilars, we include both insulins and antibodies. Insulin and insulin analogues are proteins but they are less complex proteins. They are more like long peptides. Antibodies are very complex proteins. When we talk about novel molecules, we mean oral insulin, fusion antibodies and itolizumab, an immunotherapeutic. These are the main lead molecules that we have developed and taken it into an advanced stage of development.

People have been very sceptical about our investment in biosimilars because they are very complex proteins. And making an equivalent of a complex protein, which is what biosimilars are, is a very difficult thing to do.

Unlike a conventional generic drug based on chemical molecules that are simple to copy, making a biosimilar is complex because you cannot synthesize it chemically. You have to use a living system to synthesize it and since you don't have the exact living system that the original manufacturer used, you have to develop a living system that mimics it. That is a difficult thing to do. To give a simple analogy, it is like growing tomatoes in different farms. You can clone the tomato in two farms and they can be extremely similar, but they cannot be exact replicas because the growing environments are different.

That is the challenge with biosimilars. How similar can biosimilars be to the original molecule? Both biotech companies and regulators are now getting to grips with this challenge through new technologies and analytics that can map a biosimilar with an original molecule. It's a field that is evolving very rapidly.

We are developing a portfolio of six biosimilars for oncology and autoimmune indications— trastuzumab, pegfilgrastim, adalimumab, bevacizumab, etanercept, and filgrastim; and three generic insulin analogues—glargine, lispro and aspart, in partnership with Mylan, an American pharmaceutical company. Trastuzumab and pegfilgrastim are already under review by the European drug regulator European Medicines Agency (EMA) and we also plan to file for review in the USA. Biocon obtained its first biosimilar approval in a developed country when Japan approved sales of our insulin glargine in the country through our partner FUJIFILM Pharma. Simultaneously, we are working on introducing the biosimilars in emerging markets such as Latin America, Africa, Middle East, Eastern Europe and Southeast Asia through licensing pacts with local partners.

It takes a minimum of five to six years to develop a biosimilar from start to finish and it costs anywhere from $50 to $150 million per molecule. We have taken longer because the whole area was evolving.

After several years of dealing with sceptical investors and analysts, Biocon is being recognized globally because we are seen to have a pipeline of biosimilars ready for the market. No one believed a company out of India could do it with homegrown technology and that is a great feeling.

For a long time, our stock was undervalued. I think India was just not getting the story. People kept asking us, 'Why are you investing so much in R&D? Biosimilars do not have a future. Biocon is wasting shareholder money. We are not seeing the needle move.' Etcetera, etcetera. Basically they were saying, 'We don't buy your story.'

So I told them, 'Guys, please understand. I know what I am doing. This is going to be a big story for Biocon. Don't underestimate this business.'

And sure enough, when we got the Japanese approval for our insulin glargine; people woke up and said, 'Yes, this could become big.' Then companies like Sandoz got approved for the filgrastim in Europe and US, and suddenly everybody realized that the market for biosimilars was potentially huge. Now everybody sees the biosimilars story and there are not too many people in the business, because everyone had kept saying biosimilars will never fly, it's too expensive, why invest in such a risky business?

Nobody has the stomach and the risk appetite to invest $100 million per molecule and wait out the gestational period of five to six years. So today, Biocon is the only game in town in biosimilars as far as India is concerned.

People often make the mistake of clubbing IT services and biotech when they talk about the India tech story. It is a completely wrong categorization. IT services and BPO (business process outsourcing) are predictable, low-risk businesses where you can start making money very quickly.

Biotech is a highly risky, capital-intensive, and IP-led business with long gestation times. Investors who have made easy money funding the IT services business will find it impossible to stomach the much higher risk in the biotech business.

I honestly believe that if a professional manager was running Biocon, the company would have shut shop long ago. This is a disruptive business and I can't see anyone but a promoter taking such risks.

So the question is, *how do you institutionalize this risk taking? How do you ensure that as the company grows, we don't get sidetracked by short-term opportunism?*

I try to do that through extensive communication. Most of people who work with me directly have been here for a long time and we share the same vision. I'm not exactly sure how it happens, but creating the right culture is an osmotic process. And if you can inspire your direct reports, then that culture can cascade downwards to teams reporting to them and onwards.

It hasn't been an easy journey getting to where we are at Biocon and it almost certainly will never be an easy journey at any time. This is an innovation driven, IP-led business and we need to create something new all the time. That is *both* the challenge and the reward.

Oberoi Hotels

The Oberoi Group, founded in 1934, operates thirty hotels, Nile cruisers in Egypt, and a motor vessel in the backwaters of Kerala. The group is present in six countries under the luxury Oberoi brand and the five-star Trident brand. Among the luxury Indian hotel chains, many consider the Oberoi to be the best. *Conde Nast Traveller* routinely rates Oberoi hotels among the top hotels in India, and in 2015, Oberoi Udaivilas in Udaipur was voted the second best hotel in the world. In 2014, The Oberoi Mumbai was voted the best hotel in the world by Institutional Investor magazine. In 2016, *Travel + Leisure* named Oberoi Hotels & Resorts the best hotel brand in the world for the second year in a row. The magazine quotes a guest as saying, 'Oberoi is unique in its ability to transform a busy place into a sanctuary of tranquility.'

Luxury is good business for Oberoi. In an industry suffering from the economic slowdown, EIH Ltd (FY16 revenue Rs 1816 crore, $280 million), the company that runs the Oberoi and Trident hotels, is the most profitable among the big Indian hotel chains. Among the others, ITC is profitable while Hotel Leela Venture and Indian Hotels (owners of the Taj brand) make losses.

Much of excellence can be attributed to P R S 'Biki' Oberoi (born 1929), executive chairman of EIH Ltd, and chairman of Oberoi Hotels Pvt Ltd. In 1984, he inherited the then nine-hotel chain from his father, group founder Rai Bahadur Mohan Singh Oberoi. Since then, the chain has been synonymous with luxury—much like its chairman. Biki Oberoi was educated in India, UK, and Switzerland and is known to appreciate the good life—Cohiba cigars, the best Darjeeling tea, white-gloved butlers in his homes, and black-tie parties. His attention to detail is legendary and there are stories about how the flowers in vases need to be of the perfect length, how the bath towels are measured for whiteness with a light meter, and how not just the guest rooms but also all public rooms need to be spotlessly clean at an Oberoi property.

That luxury and attention to detail was in ample evidence at our meeting in his sprawling farmhouse-cum-office in the outskirts of Delhi. Playing the perfect host, Biki Oberoi, cigar in place, reminisced about his journey and spoke about the need for his luxury hotels to adapt to an Airbnb world.

Leader speak: P R S 'Biki' Oberoi

I don't want to be the biggest hotel chain but I do want to be the best. I say that all the time. Our mantra is *guests' first, company next, self last*.

People often ask me why I am so fussy about detail. It goes back to the way I grew up. The whole family lived in hotels. I travelled a great deal in my younger days and my father encouraged me to go around the world and see different hotels. I also worked in hotels in Europe when I was in my twenties. And so I knew what a good hotel should be like.

I was very fortunate that I inherited a good business from my father. In those days, the Mandarin Oriental in Bangkok was rated the best hotel in the world. I remember my father asking me why we couldn't build hotels like that. It was a challenge and I said I will try. Then we built The Oberoi in Mumbai and it was very successful. But during the terrorist attack of November 2008, that hotel was destroyed and we had to rebuild it completely. It took us seventeen months and we spent a lot of money doing it. When it was rebuilt, it was rated as the best hotel in the world by *Institutional Investor*, the same magazine that had motivated my father to challenge us to build a great hotel all those years ago.

The hotel industry is like the airline industry in some ways. Service is what counts. Hygiene is what counts. You don't want to get into a dirty aircraft, and if you're not treated properly by the crew, it's not very pleasant. And of course the ground handling has to be right too. If the flight is delayed, you have to explain to passengers why it is delayed. A lot of airlines don't care.

At a good hotel, service is the key. You can build the best hotel but if you can't provide good service, nobody is going to come to your hotel, or very few people will come and they will complain.

So we select our people with a lot of care. We train them carefully, and you have to keep them motivated. I think that's our success. I've said that before and I'm saying it too often, maybe. People are our biggest asset.

We have our own training center to instill these high standards. The center was opened in 1966 and it offers a two year post graduate management program in guest service, housekeeping, and kitchen management.

Someone asked me, 'Why a program for housekeepers?' It's simple. A person who is attending to cleaning your room probably has never used a bed sheet at home, or washes it maybe once a week or twice a week. Our standards are that if you have a rust stain on your bed sheet and it's visible to the customer, you change the sheet, and send it back to the laundry. Our standards of housekeeping are very, *very* strict. People expect that from a luxury hotel, and if they don't like something, you'll read about it quickly in the many travel advisories today and on social media.

So you have to build a culture that values such standards and that comes from personal examples and communication. You have to be at it all the time in our business, day after day, year after year. My son is the CEO now and he visits the hotels frequently and talks to people just as I used to do till a few years back. We have captured our mission, vision, and dharma in a booklet that everyone in the hotel is deeply familiar with and follows. It is not something that came from management. I don't remember exactly when, but about fifteen years back, we had a seminar where we called a lot of our people and asked them to create a mission and vision. This is something that came from them and it is something that we believe in and work towards all the time. It is the standard to which we hold ourselves.

In the old days, when the company was much smaller, my father used to go through every complaint from the guests. I go through all the negative TripAdvisor reviews regularly. For example, someone complained that we didn't concentrate on vegetarian food and so of course we addressed that. Food is critical and the challenge in India is that it varies widely by region. And since you have to cater to widely different tastes, both the *aloo parantha* and the *dosa* that you serve in Delhi and in Chennai have to be equally good in both places even though one of them is not native to that city in each of these places.

The market is changing in many ways. Till about ten years ago, 80 per cent of our customers were foreign travellers. That has now dropped to 60 per cent and we get more and more of Indian guests. There are quite a few Indians who now think that it is okay to pay the 30,000 rupees per night or so that it costs to stay in say, an Oberoi Udaivilas. They earn in dollars, the rupee has depreciated, and having travelled and lived across the world, they know these prices are comparable to what they would pay elsewhere for the same quality.

In the hotel industry we talk about the leisure segment and the business segment but of course, people don't fall into such neat categories. Most of our guests in the big cities are business travellers. But if you come to Delhi on business, you are quite likely to travel to an Agra or a Jaipur as a tourist and your expectations from a hotel there will be different than in the metros. So we have to cater to this mix of expectations.

The troubles of 2008 have affected us and the rest of the industry. First, there was the financial meltdown in the US and then there was the terror attack in Mumbai. All of a sudden, economies everywhere slowed down and simultaneously, the world became a more uncertain place. No place is safe except home, I suppose. Anywhere you go, Paris, Istanbul, Delhi, things could get deteriorate suddenly. For example, our hotel in Egypt is not doing well because of the troubles there. We still haven't seen a pickup in business travel across our hotels. I hope things get better.

There are other changes in the industry. Business travelers are not concerned about the crystal chandeliers as they are about convenience and time. We are adapting. For example, in Mumbai, our chauffeurs can do in-car meal ordering for guests so that a meal is ready on arrival. We offer 24-hour butler service on every floor to handle guest requests. And the in-room dining menu now caters to busy guests with a new selection of smaller, simpler meals delivered in just a few minutes. And everywhere, Wi-Fi has been upgraded so that guests can be connected to the internet straightaway. Today hotels must compete with options like Airbnb (a peer-to-peer online home stay network) and even if they are not direct competitors, we must try and incorporate some of the conveniences they offer.

But of course, technology also helps us to serve guests better. Nowadays, we track everything and so we have much more information about our guests than previously. We know what they purchased, where they went, what they asked for, and so we are able to offer them a more personalized service both during their stay and when they return. It helps us customize incentive packages that are more tailored and relevant to individual tastes and lifestyles.

Technology also allows us to improve our products in new ways. For example, in April 2016, we closed The Oberoi New Delhi for renovations. It is an old property and will be renovated completely before it is opens in 2018. One of the things we plan to do is to use technology to make the air inside the hotel fresher and cleaner than it is on the outside. We have the technology to do that now and clean air in Delhi is becoming important to our guests. Our hotels have always been known for their cleanliness and improving the air quality is a natural extension.

Luxury is not just about service anymore. We also need to create exceptional experiences and memories for our guests. Everyone says that, of course, but how many hotels can do that? It's not easy unless you have exceptional people and that goes back training and culture.

Some months ago, we initiated a new *Empower* program that gives every employee a certain amount of money, or an amenity credit to give to guests as they deem fit, no questions asked. Initially, some of our team members were concerned that the program might be abused in some way, but our results show otherwise. We have seen our net promoter scores rise after implementing the program. This was one way of making every employee a brand ambassador of the hotel in a tangible way. Once you empower people and given them responsibility and start trusting them, people will embrace it.

Good service is not about getting a cup of coffee in two minutes but in how you are greeted, how you are served, how you are seated at the table. People from all over the world stay at our hotels. We want them to feel at home. That's the key. I hope that never changes at Oberoi.

Himalaya

The Himalaya Drug Company (CY16 revenue Rs 2100 crore, $320 million) manufactures and markets herbal healthcare, personal care and animal health products. The company was founded in Dehradun in 1930 by M Manal and the story goes that his first success was inspired by a trip to Burma where he saw restless elephants being calmed with some herb. That led to Serpina, the world's first herbal antihypertensive drug. In the 1950s the company moved to Mumbai and had great success with Liv.52, a liver medication. In 1975, Meraj Manal, the founder's son, started moving operations to Bengaluru. The younger Manal dreamt of taking the company global and wanted a large campus to set up an integrated facility. Today, with its modern marketing, ISO and USFDA certified facilities, and sales in over 90 countries, Himalaya is steadily building a global brand and derives over 30 per cent of its revenue from outside India.

Meraj Manal (born in 1945), chairman of Himalaya Global Holdings Ltd, the parent company of Himalaya Drug Company, is a soft spoken but restless man. Flitting between the company's offices across the world, Manal is a great believer in observation and instinct, and has little patience with committees and lengthy presentations. He is far happier communicating over a quick phone call or videoconference, or increasingly these days, over WhatsApp instant messenger.

Leader speak: Meraj Manal

When I was young and new in the company, it always bothered me that we were content to sell and grow only in India. I pleaded with my father to permit me to do something on a global scale. I felt that until we grew and proved ourselves internationally, we would just be frogs in a well.

In the seventies, after much persuasion, my father agreed to begin the move to Bengaluru from Mumbai. I wanted to build a campus-style facility that could in time house everything under one roof. I wanted a place where our research scientists, production people, quality experts, marketing gurus, and everyone else could work together in a park-like setting and create magic! That would have been impossible in Mumbai because of the prohibitive cost. Bengaluru also has the advantage of being a magnet for very smart people and that helps too.

My first trip to the USA in the seventies was a very humbling experience. The people were nice and the market opportunity was huge. But the regulatory environment was daunting. It would be another twenty years before the USFDA (Food and Drug Administration) implemented the Dietary Supplement Health and Education Act in 1994 that would pave the way for herbal products to be marketed in the country. Two years after that Act came into place, we launched our products in the USA.

But our major breakthrough came when I moved to the Cayman Islands in the late nineties and set up our first store—now fondly known as Store One—in the capital, George Town. Cayman is two and a half hours from Houston, Texas, and is one of the world's most interesting melting pots. People from all over the world come there for business and pleasure. I worked in the store for two years and it was an extraordinary opportunity to get to know and observe the wide variety of people who came and shopped at the store. I was getting the most direct feedback I could have hoped for from one of the most varied and diverse customer bases anywhere in the world.

At that time, Himalaya was a herbal pharmaceutical company. While our drugs were flying off the shelves, I kept getting inquiries for herbal soaps, shampoos, lotions and other wellness and cosmetic products. 'You are a herbal company,' people kept telling me. 'So why don't you make shampoos and other stuff?'

I realized we were ignoring a huge market opportunity. People take medicines when they are unwell; but they consume personal care and wellness products all the time. So I talked to our research people in India and got them excited about making herbal FMCG (fast moving consumer goods) and wellness products.

It was a crazy arrangement. This was before the internet, and I would spend a small fortune each month on international calls talking to the R&D team in Bengaluru about the market insights I was getting in the Caymans. In response, they would create and FedEx me samples of products. In some cases, these products were formulations we already had. For example, we repurposed toothpowder formulations that we had in my father's library and produced them as toothpaste. At other times, we created products for which we had the recipe but had never considered to produce.

Cayman is a small place and the word spread. Someone said the bleeding in his gums stopped after using our toothpaste and that brought new customers to the store. Feedback helped to continuously improve the products, and our concept of head-to-heel wellness took shape over the next couple of years.

Cayman was also a fantastic launch pad in other ways. When I first entered the market and wanted to create awareness, I took out a centre spread advertisement in the widely read local paper, *Cayman Compass*. The campaign ran for several weeks and created a splash. Customers flocked to the store. The medical fraternity took umbrage and complained. So one day, the then Minister of Health came to the store, bought some cough syrup, and told me to go easy on the advertising since it was riling the local doctors. We complied, and that was it.

That was the wonderful thing about Cayman. It was such a small and open place that there was virtually no bureaucracy. If the government wanted to tell you something, they told you, and that was it. No notices, no litigation, no rancour. I would have never had that kind of freedom to expand our product range or explore new methods of marketing in almost any other country. The Cayman Islands have been good for Himalaya.

The same lack of bureaucracy has worked wonders for us elsewhere. As we continue to expand globally, the company is structured to grow through subsidiaries, each serving a country or a region. India is our oldest unit and will continue to be central to our growth. But we now have a major presence in Dubai, Houston, Singapore, Poland, and other places. Each of these business units will eventually be self-contained entities with their own research, production, and marketing. In each case, we've been pleasantly surprised by the ease of doing business.

One of the big learnings from going global is the importance of research, quality, and branding. From our beginnings in the 1930s when our founder created a tablet from the *rauwolfia serpentina* root, Himalaya has been science-led. That approach has been refined and strengthened over the years as we have prepared the company and our processes to comply with regulatory and certification standards in all the countries in which we operate. In fact, during a recent visit to our Bengaluru plant, a USFDA inspector told us that it was one of the best ones he had seen in our line of work. We told him that we are in the process of building an even better one!

Our approach to branding was also a consequence of going global. Our early successes were all based on product brands. People knew Serpina was for hypertension, Liv.52 was for the liver, Cystone was for kidney stones, and so on. The product brands were immensely popular and continue to be so.

But as our product portfolio grew to the hundreds and as we expanded into multiple geographies, we needed to unify these products under one brand. So in the early 2000s, we used the company name as an umbrella and created the Himalaya brand and logo. The project was brilliantly conceived and executed by Bengaluru-based agency Ray+Keshavan, and today, the distinctive teal and orange Himalaya logo is visible and recognized in over ninety countries. I've had people across the world come up to me at airports on seeing the logo on my luggage tag, strike up a conversation, and affectionately talk about the number of Himalaya products used in their family. God bless them!

We have an internal target to grow to $1 billion in global revenue by 2020. We are currently close to $450 million globally which means we need to grow at about 22 per cent per year for the next few years. Achievable!

I have never been a big believer in analysis paralysis. I believe that a committee is good at keeping minutes but wastes hours. Instead, I tend to manage by observation and instinct. Of course we have processes, and each of our business units are run by professional CEOs who monitor metrics and keep track of the numbers. But I see my role as the chairman to keep the big picture alive and to make the calls that are not always supported by short-term profit considerations. It helps that we are a private company. I have the freedom to plan for the long-term without being pressured by quarterly targets or a share price.

All innovation begins with observation. My father's observation of elephants in Burma started it all for us. As a schoolboy, I would accompany my father to visit his friend at the large and sprawling headquarters of the Glaxo pharmaceutical company in Worli, Mumbai. I was always fascinated by the thought of how much work went on in such a large building and I am convinced that my move from Mumbai to Bengaluru was subliminally influenced by the belief that we too would need to think this big if we were serious about growing our business.

The expansion of our portfolio from pharmaceuticals to personal care, animal health, and wellness was based on what I observed in the Cayman Islands.

Each of our moves to global locations was based on our sense of the opportunities and ease of doing business in those countries.

This sense of being guided by observation drills down to product design too. For example, I once observed during a family lunch at a restaurant in Mumbai that one of the girls went up to her mother and whispered something in her ear. I have a knack of sizing up a situation and I figured the girl was experiencing menstrual cramps and was too shy to take a tablet with a glass of water in public. I later confirmed this with her mother. In response, we developed a chewable gel tablet that quickly dissolves in the mouth. It is discreet, effective, and is in the last stages of testing.

Or take the case of our recent line of hand sanitizers in multiple fruit fragrances. It was based on our observation that people are increasingly aware of the connection between clean hands and common infections. They want something that is convenient and smells fresh and natural. Sure enough, the product line is a big hit.

Sometimes, this sense of observation works in reverse. There was a wonderful product that our R&D team developed recently. It was a chewable, self-dissolving tablet that could replace toothpaste. We didn't proceed with it because I felt people needed the tactile sensation of brushing their teeth. I just could not bring myself to give the go-ahead, and the project was dropped.

Many of our products are not the result of conventional market research. They are born out of what I, or someone in my team, feels is an opportunity. And when we sense an opportunity, we do not skimp on resources. We have virtually no cap on R&D costs. If a product or an opportunity looks promising, we are prepared to invest in it significantly. Our goal is that all research must result in affordable products.

It's the same with our geographical expansion. In many countries, we do small volumes of business. It doesn't matter. Building a brand takes a long time, and we are prepared for the long haul if we think that market has potential.

Make no mistake. Building an international brand is tough. There are barriers due to regulations, due to language, and due to culture. I've had my fair share of critics who have sneered at our efforts. When I was building the business in Cayman and elsewhere, I've had people come up to me and say, 'Oh, are you another motel Patel from India?'

You have to believe in yourself to get through the negativity. My response to people who talk about shoddy products coming out of India is to build products and to build a company that is not shoddy. It doesn't matter who the competitors are. Competitors come and go all the time; it is a free market out there. As for the naysayers, it doesn't matter what they say. The world is a large place and there are more than seven billion people in it. I neither intend to, nor can possibly sell to all of them. All I hope is that a fraction of them sees value in using our products.

At the end of the day, it is about respect. We are going to get this right because it is a matter of pride to me and my team that as Indians, we should stand out. I am driven to see that our products should shine. And when we get acknowledgement of that from customers in countries around the world, I feel good. It goes back to why I started to go global in the first place. We shouldn't have to settle for being a big frog in a small well. We should aim to be recognized in the whole wide world.

We're getting there.

Narayana Health

Narayana Hrudayalaya Ltd (FY16 revenue Rs 1617 crore, $250 million), which operates under the Narayana Health brand, is a healthcare chain of twenty-three hospitals, seven heart centers, and a network of primary care facilities across India, and one hospital in the Cayman Islands. Narayana Health has a strong legacy in cardiac, renal, and neuro sciences, a strong presence in Karnataka and eastern India, and an emerging presence in western and central India. The flagship hospital in Bengaluru is famous for low-cost, high-volume heart surgeries. The Wall Street Journal called Dr Devi Prasad Shetty, the founder and chairman, 'the Henry Ford of heart surgery' and Bloomberg called the hospital 'the Walmart of heart surgery' and with good reason. When it comes to high-volume, low-cost heart surgery, Narayana Health is the world leader. Cleveland Clinic in Ohio, the leading heart programme center in the USA conducts about 2500 heart surgeries a year. The Fortis Escorts Heart Institute in Delhi, a leading cardiac center in India, conducts about 3200 heart surgeries per year. Narayana Health has performed 127,000 heart surgeries in the last fifteen years. That is an average of 8,460 per year. And they have brought down the cost of a cardiac bypass to 100,000 rupees without sacrificing anything by way of clinical quality. They do this through relentless process innovation.

Dr Devi Shetty (born 1953), is a pleasant, and soft-spoken man who says his early training in the martial arts helps him get through the gruelling 18-hour workdays. After returning from the UK, he initially worked in Kolkata and it was there that he both treated and was deeply inspired by Mother Teresa. Dr Shetty was one of my most transparent interviewees. His office responded quickly to a meeting request, set it up without fuss, and reverted quickly when I followed up for clarification and data. This is his story.

Leader speak: Dr Devi Shetty

I strongly believe that India will become the first country in the world to dissociate healthcare from affluence. When I was a medical student, everyone told us that healthcare will always be expensive. But one day we will become a rich country, and then all of us can afford healthcare.

But when we grew up, we looked at the richest countries of the world like America and England and saw them struggling to offer healthcare to their citizens. It became clear to me that however rich India becomes, we will not be able to provide affordable healthcare unless we change the model of delivering it.

Why is this important? Because a critical heart operation is non-negotiable. If I charge a poor man a price for his surgery that he cannot afford, I am indirectly writing his death sentence. That has to change.

We have made a change. The first patient on whom I performed a cardiac bypass surgery in India was in Kolkata in 1990 and he paid 160,000 rupees. More than twenty-five years later today at Narayana, we are doing the same operation for 100,000 rupees. Show me one other service that has reduced the price to this level over a twenty-five-year period.

But reducing cost is only one part of the problem. You also have to create a capacity to pay. We have addressed both problems. As a healthcare provider, we work to reduce the cost of surgery to the bare minimum. And we work with governments to create the capacity to pay. Let me tell you how.

Micro insurance to create payment capacity

A vast number of our people cannot afford heart surgery. So in 2003 or so, we approached the government in Karnataka and proposed a micro health insurance scheme. It was a completely new concept then. Today, the Yeshasvini Scheme, as it is called, is one of the largest self funded healthcare schemes in India covering the rural population in Karnataka. In the first year we had 17 lakh farmers paying five rupees per month. Now we have close to 35 lakh farmers paying about 25 rupees per month. Beneficiaries can avail cashless treatment for over 800 surgical procedures across a network of over 475 hospitals. In the last ten years close to 10 lakh farmers have had various surgeries, and over one lakh farmers have had a heart operation. (1 lakh = 100,000)

Other state governments in South India have launched similar schemes. Millions of people are getting benefited. Think about it. We have over one billion mobile phone subscribers in India and each one spends about 100 to 200 rupees a month on phone calls. If you collect just twenty or thirty rupees from each mobile phone subscriber, you have covered the surgical expense of one billion people. When one billion people can pay for surgeries, be assured that hospitals will come up all over the country to service the demand. And the demand is immense. India requires 65 million surgeries a year and we do just about 22 or 24 million.

There is an added benefit. When the hospitals come up, because people would have the capacity to pay for surgeries, there will be huge collateral benefit in all areas of medical care since setting up a surgical unit automatically ensures attendant infrastructure such as CT scanners, MRI, cath labs and other testing and imaging equipment.

Relentless innovation to reduce healthcare costs

There is no big bang approach to reducing cost in healthcare. You have to do many things, some small, some big, some disruptive.

From the outset we realized that we have to build economies of scale. As you do more operations, your results will get better. And as you do more operations, you need more equipment and supplies. As a group, we do about 45 heart surgeries a day, about 10 per cent of all heart surgeries in India. That is a powerful incentive for companies to supply us equipment and material at favourable prices.

- **Buildings.** Our innovation starts right from the building of our hospitals. We have maybe 100 towns in India with a population of half a million to one million where there are no speciality hospitals. They cannot afford a conventional modern hospital. So we approached Larsen & Toubro and told them that we want a 300-bed hospital with equipments for doing heart surgeries, brain surgeries, and cancer surgeries. But we told them that we can only pay six million dollars and we want it done in six months. L&T responded magnificently. Our hospital in Mysuru was built to these specifications and has been working brilliantly for over three years now. We cut costs by building the hospital in one storey, eliminated lifts, and consuming minimum electricity. We call it the asset-light model.

- **Materials.** At other times, we disrupt the supply chain. Take the case of the drapes and gowns used during surgery. Most hospitals in India—and I mean over 99 per cent—use linen drapes and gowns because they are cheap and can be washed and reused. But washing and reusing linen is dangerous since it carries the risk of infection from the previous operation. For this reason, linen is banned in the US and Western Europe.

  About four or five years ago, we decided to eliminate linen drapes and gowns and follow the international best practice of using disposable drapes and gowns. Considering our high volume of surgeries, linen was an unacceptable risk.

  When we looked around, we discovered that two big multinational companies had a monopoly on the supply of disposable drapes and gowns. They wanted 5,000 rupees per operation; we offered 2,500 rupees. We were then paying 1,800 rupees for linen drapes and gowns. We were prepared to pay higher for disposable drapes and gowns but the asking rate was beyond us. We pointed out that if they supplied us, they would straightaway gain 10 per cent of the market. They refused.

  So we looked for alternatives and worked with local entrepreneurs. Turns out that irrespective of who supplies the disposable drapes and gowns, the basic material was supplied by just one company. All that the suppliers did was to cut, stitch, and sterilize it. That was something we could also do, surely? So these young people set up a company called Amaryllis and took six months to understand how things work. Today, Amaryllis supplies us disposable drapes and gowns at 900 rupees per operation and they have become the number one surgical disposable company in India. The story doesn't end there. Amyrallis has applied for US FDA and European certifications and when that comes through, they will start exports and reduce our cost even further, to maybe 600 rupees per operation.
- **Care Companion.** Sometimes, you can reduce costs by incorporating the patient's family into the process. This is what we have done with our Care Companion program. Across the world,

when a patient gets admitted for a heart operation, the spouse stays with the patient. But they are not allowed to touch the patient for the four or five days he is in the hospital. Then on the sixth day we call the wife, give her a bag with all the medicines, and tell her that she should now take care of her husband.

She is lost. She doesn't know what to do with him. So what we did was to include her in providing care from the beginning so that there is continuity at home. If you think about it, there are only twelve tasks you need to teach a caregiver. Check blood pressure, check pulse rate, dress the wound, give medicines on time, physiotherapy, and so on. Digital meters make it easy to take blood pressure and measure pulse rate, and everything else can be taught. So we do that. We also make a one-minute film and load it on the spouse's phone, if they have one. Now when they go home, there is continuity of care. Readmission rate comes down significantly. And there is very high satisfaction among the patients.

- **Bedsores.** Let me end with one last example. Bedsores, or hospital acquired pressure ulcers. The incidence of bedsores following heart operation across the world is anywhere from 7 per cent to 40 per cent. We do close to 700 heart surgeries a month. If we go by that norm and accept that even 10 per cent of our patients would develop bedsores, we would need a separate building for taking care of the bedsore afflicted patients. So we decided to eliminate bedsores. And we did that by educating our staff, modifying workflows and processes, and bringing in accountability.

  It works like this. We monitor a patient through his or her movement in the hospital from the ward to the operation theater to the intensive care unit. At every location, the nursing and support staff are accountable—if they introduce a bedsore, they have to cure it. We have identified and fixed all the known causes of bedsores. It could be due to a wrinkled mattress. It could be because the patient was not turned over in bed. It could be because of a damp sheet. Little things that can be fixed, and they do get fixed, if you are held accountable. The result is that our incidence of bedsores is virtually zero. In fact, our protocol to prevent bedsores has been recognized and published in the American Nursing Journal as a benchmark.

Why healthcare matters

The biggest danger for us is not an external aggressor or some world changing event. The biggest danger for India is that one million job seekers enter the market every month and we simply are not creating enough jobs to employ even a fraction of them. Technology makes the problem worse. Take the IT industry as an example. To generate revenue of one crore rupees, a software services company needs just four or five employees. And these employees are highly educated and skilled people. In healthcare on the other hand, we require at least 250 employees to generate a revenue of one crore rupees and most of them are semi-skilled or unskilled women. At one point, about 90 per cent of Narayanas's 14,000 workforce were women. This is highly desirable. If you empower women, they teach their children to make the right choices in life and that creates a better society. I strongly believe that healthcare can not only generate massive employment but can also play a great role in stabilizing society. Governments everywhere would be wise to do more to support this industry.

Managing expectations

Narayana Hospitals is not a charity; it is a public limited company. Charity money is good to demonstrate a concept. But to grow and scale a concept, you need investors and that means that you need to run your operation embracing all the aspects of a good business—you need to deliver superior patient satisfaction, deliver adequate return on investment, and demonstrate high corporate governance.

We set up Narayana Hospitals because we see immense opportunities in affordable healthcare. There is much to do. We want to add thousands of beds both within and outside India. We are already strong in cardiac care, renal care, oncology, neurology, and neurosurgery and we want to add more specialities. To do all of this requires considerable investment and being a listed company gives current and potential investors a great deal of reassurance—they can simply go to our website or read our annual report to know everything about us. For me personally, nothing has changed since we went public. We are not sellers and our investors are with us for the long term.

Fabindia

Fabindia Overseas Pvt Ltd (FY16 revenue Rs 1148 crore, $175 million) began in 1960 as a company exporting home furnishings, set up its first retail store in New Delhi in 1975, and was creating a name for itself by the early eighties for its ethnic Indian garments made from hand-woven and hand-printed fabrics.

The company added non-textile products in 2000, organic foods in 2004, personal products in 2006, and handcrafted jewellery in 2008. Today Fabindia has a near cult following, has over 200 stores across India and stores in Singapore, Dubai, Italy, Nepal, Malaysia, and Mauritius and is the largest private platform in India for products based on traditional crafts and knowledge. Much of these are sourced from villages and the company works closely with over 55,000 artisans, providing various inputs including design, quality control, access to finance and raw materials. Fabindia plans to expand into agriculture and wellness in the near future and says all of its work is an extension of its vision of 'celebrating India'.

William Bissell (born 1966), the managing director, is a soft-spoken man and an interesting mix. He has a degree in political science from Wesleyan University, had worked as a journalist, environmentalist, and political intern and had set up a trust for artisans before joining Fabindia in 1994. He took over in 1999 after the founder, his father John Bissell, died. We met on a drizzly evening at his *barsati* (rooftop room) of an office above the Khan Market store in New Delhi. Bissell is as comfortable about talking about his network of village artisans as he is about an Infosys or a GE or his slightly mystical nine energies approach to management. This is his story.

Leader speak: William Bissell

I'd say the elements of sustained performance are quite similar across businesses. One is culture. The other is strong product demand and desirability. The two work together.

Culture is what helps you attract and retain loyalty. It's about processes. It's about the kind of people your organization attracts, recruits, and retains. It's about environment you provide to people once they come in to the company.

You can have highly desirable products but if you have a terrible culture in the organization, it's not going to sustain. Likewise, you can have an organization with a fantastic culture and processes and all of that, but if your products aren't compelling then again, your business won't sustain.

In addition to a good culture and desirable products, all companies, big or small, should have what I call, 'nine energies'. I rate these energies on a scale from zero to ten, the higher the better. It's not the overall score that matters; what matters is that no energy should be less than four or five. It's much better to have all the nine energies at a five each than to have four energies at ten and the rest at two or three. The nine energies and my rating of how we score on them at Fabindia are as follows.

- **Visionary:** This is the energy that some people possess to see the big picture and to have a vision for the future and for their enterprise. This is very important and I'd say we score a comfortable nine on this.
- **Strength of demand:** This is critical in realizing your vision because many visions can be based on products, ideas, or services that lack sufficient strength of demand. I'd say we score a six on this. We are preparing to launch a few new concepts and products and that will most likely move this score further up.
- **Conversion/planning:** This is about how you convert your vision into an actionable plan with all its components and detailing. Having a vision without a plan to realize it means that the vision will remain a dream. I'd give us a score of nine on this. We've been historically strong in this area and we're putting in place a new planning system to nurture that strength.

- **Rigor/execution:** This is the discipline of being able to convert a plan into tangible action on the ground. This is what creates a high performance organization. We should score an eight or nine here since we're good at working out key performance areas to realize an objective and continuously refining them.
- **Monitoring:** In any plan however big or small, you need to keep track of all the ratios, the performance indicators, and work towards staying close to the optimum figures. Every successful organization will score high on this. I'd give us an eight.
- **Strategic energy:** This is the energy that helps companies in making the 'chess board moves' to accelerate, make alliances, identify synergies, and look for impact. This is the energy that can take one plus one and make eleven. But that can only happen when the four preceding energies are in place. I would say this energy for us has come down from a high to maybe a four or five because the person who does all our strategy retired recently and so we'll go through a dip before we ramp up again. We've traditionally been strong in this area.
- **Conservation/balance:** This is the energy that's often missing in lot of startups that get external funding. It's the ability to remain frugal even when you have resources. It's the energy that helps an organization to conserve its strength. It goes beyond just keeping a tight control on expenses. It's a whole approach to how you execute a plan, how you avoid flab, how to be lean. This energy is key to sustainable profits. We've dropped from eight to three in this area because we've let ourselves slip a bit, we had become a little spendthrift. We're correcting that.
- **Ability to create brand awareness:** This refers to the marketing energy, the ability to network, connect, create a buzz. I'm concerned about this right now. We've dropped from a six to maybe three and so we are retooling our whole marketing plan. What used to work in the past no longer does. Take advertising for example. Earlier, we'd just run a small advert in the paper and sales would double in the next few days. Today, even a quarter page advert gets very little result. The environment has changed and we need to figure out how to cope. We're on the job.
- **Ability of the management to listen:** This is the ability of management to listen to others and to change their behavior

in response. It is about humility. I'd peg us at four to five. We've validated this recently through a third party survey.

So three of our nine energies are in the three-to-four range and the rest are in good shape. We have some work to do.

As a company, we need to keep track of not just how we are doing on a day-to-day basis, but also step back occasionally and see where we want to go. It comes back to what your vision is, what you want to be.

One way to look at business is to say that it fills a market need. Take a pizza delivery business, for example. There is a strong demand for pizza. India is urbanizing, more people are staying alone, home delivered food is convenient, cheese is tasty, etcetera, etcetera. Pizza fulfils that need perfectly. It is convenient, clean, tasty, and delivered hot in thirty minutes.

The other way to look at business is to see it as something that has a purpose, something that is trying to change the world in its own little way. That's how we see ourselves at Fabindia.

So when we put out a new product or offering, we ask ourselves if it can make a difference to the lives of the villagers that we source from. Our recent expansion into organic agriculture and Ayurveda are all part of that piece. In agriculture, we work with farmers through contract farming and in Ayurveda, we work with products and providers of indigenous health and beauty treatments to include them in the wellness revolution.

We like our business to have a strong social mission; we want to be purpose driven. So our businesses are all rooted in celebrating India, be it the crafts of India, the traditions of India, the food of India—there's lots to celebrate. Call it our differentiator, call it our vision. We stick to one kind of thing, we don't do many things. We cannot offer you bhangra and pop and disco and rap, we just do just one kind of music.

So while the world may see some of our products as unrelated diversification, to us they are part of what we have always wanted to do. It's just that we took time to build the capability to offer that product. Our move to organic foods is an example. When we first started selling produce, people told me they didn't see the rationale of buying food in a garments store. They said, 'Do you think I'll buy my *kurtas* and *kaddus* (pumpkin) from the same place?'

But it works. There is more reason to come into the store now. I now see a family stroll in and there is something for everyone from clothes to furnishings to organic produce to jewellery to cosmetics, and so on. Our stores are in prime locations and rentals are high. We need to innovate constantly to keep sales high and profits sustainable.

Culture is a big part of how we run the company. It's an ecosystem of how you work with people, how you relate to people. Culture can do wonders. Apple under Steve Jobs created not just the iPhone but an iLife.

That is a challenge many companies face. How do you continually innovate and make orbital changes? How do you avoid the plague of incrementalism?

I worry about where Fabindia will be ten years from now. I want it to be twice as desirable to customers as it is now. That means reinventing ourselves to stay relevant and compelling.

How should we grow? That question engages me and it should engage every other business owner. Because committees cannot provide vision. Committees can manage effectively, they can allocate resources intelligently, but they cannot build disruptive companies.

It's not as though big companies can't disrupt and win. Skunk Works (run by Lockheed Martin) and the old Bell Labs produced great stuff. But there was a culture that produced them and that culture is now rare in large corporations. How many big companies today have the characters and the mavericks that produced a Skunk Works? Disruptors do not fit corporate moulds. In their rush to create good team players, big companies churn out executives that look like corporate cut outs.

So how do you stay creative and innovative as you grow? Will Apple, Google, and Facebook be the same without the founders? Can creativity and innovation be institutionalized? That is a question that should bother any entrepreneur, big or small.

Paytm

Paytm (an acronym for Pay Through Mobile), one of the stars of India's ecommerce revolution, is the flagship brand of One97 Communications Ltd (FY16 revenue Rs 920 crore, $141 million). It was set up in 2011 as a mobile recharge business, is now a leading player in mobile payments and O2O (online-to-offline) ecommerce, and plans to expand into financial services.

The payment business began as a digital wallet. Registered users can use it in lieu of cash to transact with registered merchants to shop, pay bills, recharge mobiles and data cards, transfer money, buy movie tickets, bus and other tickets, pay taxi and auto fares, and so on. The business grows as more merchants and customers register with Paytm and transaction volumes grow. Paytm makes money by charging a commission from the merchants and earning interest on the money in the digital wallets. By early 2017, Paytm had over 150 million registered users and claimed to be India's biggest digital wallet company.

But digital wallets have a drawback. Consumers don't earn interest on the money and they can't withdraw it as cash. So when the Reserve Bank of India invited applications for licenses to set up payment banks, Paytm was an early applicant. In January 2017, One97 received approval and moved its wallets business to Paytm Payments Bank.

A payment bank is a bank with restricted banking functions. It can accept deposits, offer payments and remittance services and internet banking, but cannot lend money. But it can generate income through financial and banking products.

Paytm plans to expand aggressively into small towns to grow its customer base. It also plans to offer wealth management tools and money market funds with high liquidity to make its payment bank more attractive than a savings account in a conventional bank.

The Paytm ecommerce play is different from the warehouse led model of other ecommerce players like Amazon, Flipkart, and Snapdeal. Unlike them, Paytm is a pure marketplace. It provides a platform for merchants and it's up to the merchant to deliver the product to the consumer. Paytm charges the merchants a commission and is actively pursuing the O2O (online-to-offline) model where a consumer can shop for a product on the website and purchase it from a local shop.

By mid 2016, including recharges, wallets, and ecommerce, Paytm had notched up Rs 2,000 crore in gross merchandise value (GMV, or cost of goods and services sold) placing it alongside larger rivals, Flipkart and Amazon India.

Vijay Shekhar Sharma (born 1978), chairman and managing director of One97 Communications, set up the company in 2000 and has pivoted many times. One97 began as a people search service for mobile operators, then provided value-added content services like cricket and Bollywood news to mobile phone companies, became a prepaid phone service app, and ultimately settled on the Paytm platform. Investors in the company include Ant Financial (an affiliate of Alibaba, the Chinese ecommerce giant), SAIF Partners, and others.

Sharma, an alumnus of the Delhi College of Engineering, is the quintessential entrepreneur. His difficult journey from having no money to pay for rent or food to being one of the poster boys of India's ecommerce revolution (Paytm was reportedly valued at $5 billion during a round of funding in August 2016) is a story that is admiringly told and retold in the startup community.

I met Sharma in his chaotic office in a dusty part of Noida, outside Delhi. There is a slogan in huge letters on the wall that says, *Go Big or Go Home*. Speaking passionately and rapidly in an accent that unabashedly combines the earthy cadences of his native Aligarh with the Americanized English of the tech entrepreneur, Sharma makes it clear that he is not going home anytime soon.

Leader speak: Vijay Shekhar Sharma

Paytm began life as a mobile wallet by enabling consumers to recharge their mobile phones. A large number of consumers would recharge their phones frequently with small amounts, say, 100 or 200 rupees per transaction. These small-value high-volume transactions were of little interest to the banks or the telcos. It was tedious for them to track and reverse a transaction when it failed due to erratic connectivity. We offered a no-questions-asked refund and soon built up a large and loyal customer base. As we grew this customer base, we were able to monitor and track consumer behavior and create highly targeted offerings based on a consumer's buying behavior, credit history, and tastes. As we evolve from a digital wallet company to a payments bank, our range of offerings will extend from the present recharges and purchases to loans to mutual funds, insurance, and other financial services products. The growing customer base is also a powerful incentive for more merchants to join our market place in our ecommerce business.

Why do we spend so much on advertising?

In 2015, Paytm spent over 200 crore rupees to win the title sponsorship rights for Indian cricket for four years. We also launched multiple other business support campaigns across different divisions such as electricity bill payment, bus ticketing, and offline payments vertical. We have publicly said that we intend to spend 600 crore rupees on branding and communication in FY 2016-17.

People ask me why we spend so much on advertising and brand building. To understand this, you have to understand how we grew.

For the first ten years of our journey from 2000 onwards, we piggybacked on mobile phone companies by providing recharge services and value-added content services. The telcos paid us a percentage of their revenue and as they added customers, our revenue increased. So we did not need to spend on marketing to grow our brand; we simply grew with the telcos.

But when the smartphone arrived and people started accessing the internet on their phones, it was time for us to reach the consumer directly and build our brand independently. We could no longer piggyback on the telcos.

So the high visibility that you see these days is a necessary expense to acquire a critical mass of customers. We believe 80 per cent of consumption on the internet in India will be done by about 120 million people. But to ensure a good percentage of that 120 million, we need to win a much larger customer base. We believe that figure is around 500 million and so that's our goal.

We have a customer base of over 150 million now and so you will continue to see a fairly aggressive spend on brand building and customer acquisition activities for some time to come. And since cricket and Bollywood are the simplest ways to reach people in large numbers in India, you will see us prominently in those areas.

Managing exponential growth

We are growing rapidly. In the early years, we were doubling and tripling our headcount every year, and by March 2016, we had grown to 5,000 people and that growth continues.

High-growth companies like ours in new business areas have to do several things well at the same time to sustain a healthy culture.

Our business requires continually on-boarding customers and merchants. Hence, as an organization we need to be extremely sensitive to feedback from the market. For example, no amount of discussion will give you insight into what will make it easier for a taxi or auto rickshaw driver to come onboard with us. You need to prioritize the inputs from the person who is signing them on, the people in the field.

So we tend to build teams based on need and not on hierarchy. This customer-centricity means that we triangulate insights from the field in many ways—we send independent market research teams to gather data, we frequently send design teams to the field, and of course, we listen carefully to the business development teams to arrive at products and processes that make it easy for customers to join us and engage with us.

High growth at scale also means that our organization structure is a flexible open-ended entity. I call it the 'amoeba organization' because it changes shape around people and process requirements. We can't have an organization where reporting hierarchies impede efficiency. There are the small but significant behaviour changes that contribute to this culture. For example, I sit with the team in an open office. It is a powerful signal that hierarchies shouldn't hinder efficiency and communication.

We also have an incredibly open culture where debate is encouraged. You simply can't run a technology intensive business if someone who is junior but technically savvy cannot speak out and point out a flaw or a much needed process or product improvement. And because these conversations can sometimes be difficult and seemingly antagonistic because you may be upsetting someone's apple cart, we have a culture where it is okay to speak out. We let it be known widely that the intention is not to pull down a team or a person but to improve a product or process. You have to send out a clear message that the organization comes first.

As a founder you have to be clear about what you bring to the table in high growth companies. One of the things you need to do is to let go as the business matures. There are parts of the business at Paytm that I don't run anymore. We have a content business, a marketing business, a cloud business and I don't head them anymore. They have a business model, and they have competent leaders. As a founder, my only challenge there is to stay connected so that they don't feel abandoned by the leadership.

I want to build a company where my teammates in charge of a line of business can say, 'Vijay, we will take this business to one billion; we will make it international.' I believe we have that mojo in the company because everyone feels involved, they feel they are part of something big. In a 15-year old company, that is no accident.

We are a company that is bubbling with entrepreneurial energy because everybody wants to create something. I tell them, 'This is your life. I will provide the platform, the office, the tea and snacks, and a brand. So go ahead and develop something that will enrich and satisfy both you and the company.'

That's how I see Paytm growing. I believe the role of a founder is to champion new businesses. In our case, we have a long, hard road ahead of us to grow the payments business and the ecommerce business and I expect to stay engaged for the long term. But as these business gain traction, they will be managed by extremely competent people and not by me.

As they say, Amazon does not need a Jeff Bezos for what it is doing *now*. Amazon needs Jeff Bezos for what it is *not* doing now. That is the role of a founder. To take risks, to disrupt, to innovate. Let me put it this way. If the role of management is to take care of the percentage and grow the rupee, the role of the founder is to seek new opportunities and grow the multiple.

chlorophyll

chlorophyll, spelled in the lower case to underline its belief that while people may be unequal as professionals, they are equal as human beings, calls itself India's first end-to-end brand consultancy. The work includes creating new brands, changing existing brands, and adapting international brands to India. The company has defined and differentiated more than 200 brands to date.

Madan Bahal and Kiran Khalap co-founded chlorophyll in 1999 and the late Anand Halve joined them later. Khalap (born 1958), the soft-spoken managing director, is partial to a clean-shaven head, open collar shirts, and jackets. He began life as a teacher in a J Krishnamurthi Foundation school, rose to become CEO at Clarion, one of India's oldest advertising agencies, and now juggles spiritual evolution, writing, and rock climbing.

Leader speak: Kiran Khalap

Later in this story, I'll talk about the chlorophyll approach to branding in terms of our framework. But let me start with a specific example where we used much of that approach in the specific case of a company rebrand. It grounds the discussion in reality, something that marketing and advertising people are often accused of not doing!

In 2013, we pitched for and won the account to rebrand Quest Global Manufacturing. Quest Manufacturing was then part of Quest Global, a midsized Indian multinational engineering services company that counted GE and Rolls Royce as clients and offered a portfolio of engineering services.

In recent years, Quest Global had forayed into manufacturing for aerospace, oil and gas, and automotive customers. Their reasoning was that manufacturing was a logical step up on the engineering value chain. To support this expansion, Aravind Melligeri, one of the co-founders of Quest Global, had invested in a special economic zone (SEZ) in Belagavi in north Karnataka and was developing it as a precision manufacturing hub.

A few years into the diversification, however, the promoters decided to segregate the manufacturing business from the engineering business. Manufacturing was capital intensive and attracted a different profile of customers, employees, and investors from engineering services.

By the time we entered the picture, Aravind had spun off the manufacturing and SEZ business but was still operating under the Quest umbrella. He now wanted to create an independent company and brand.

A company rebrand is a significant event. You need systematic research to reveal the DNA of a company, and you need creativity to translate that research into a new identity. Vijay Menon, who was the marketing consultant hired by Aravind to manage the project, calls it 'part process, part magic.'

chlorophyll's approach to creating a brand is based on identifying and describing three components that we call the Brand Core, brand communication, and brand behaviour.

The Brand Core is an idea at the heart of a brand that does not change with time. James Bond is a good example. While very different actors have played the role of the fictional secret agent, the core idea of a suave, alpha male Lothario remains constant.

The brand communication is the set of text and visuals to describe the brand. This includes the logo, typography, taglines, style manual, advertising, and so on.

The brand behaviour converts the brand values into day-to-day behavior for everyone from the factory floor to corner offices.

Uncovering the Brand Core

Uncovering the brand core is all about getting people to open up to you. We gathered the senior management in a room and queried them on how they viewed themselves and how they thought their customers viewed them. The conversation was unhurried but focused.

We then took time to mull over the findings and went back to the client with two options for the brand core.

Option one was that Quest Manufacturing was a company that used every engagement with clients to symbiotically learn and scale up in skills, expertise, and process refinement. In this version, the Brand Core was that co-creation creates an upward spiral of value creation.

Option two was that Quest Manufacturing believed in a collaborative approach to manufacturing. It recognized that manufacturing was a complex set of interconnected processes and no one company could ever hope to do it all. So Quest Manufacturing worked to acquire expertise in some areas, and collaborated with partners in other areas to extend their range. For example, at the Belagavi SEZ, Quest Manufacturing had set up joint ventures with various global companies for specialized surface treatments, assembly, forging, and other processes. This meant that customers didn't have to go anywhere else after a part was machined at Quest.

Validating the Brand Core

To validate the two brand core options, we talked to internal stakeholders (employees) and external stakeholders (customers, partners, and investors).

When the interviews were done, it was clear that Option two overwhelmingly resonated with both internal and external audiences. More than 70 per cent of employees and customers agreed that collaboration was at the heart of Quest Manufacturing's promise. Customers spoke about the willingness and the ability of managers at all levels to listen and learn, and they appreciated the efforts that the company had taken to develop a manufacturing ecosystem at the SEZ.

Brand context

Having identified and validated the Brand Core, we went on to create a context and structure for the brand. This is a mental construct to understand how a brand can deliver on its promise.

At the top of this structure is the customer proposition—what a brand offers its consumers. Underlying the customer proposition is the Brand Territory, the competitive space the brand occupies. At the base is the Brand Core, the central idea driving the business. Supporting the customer proposition, and grounded in the brand core, are one or more pillars, distinguishing characteristics or strengths of the brand.

In the case of Quest Manufacturing, the customer proposition was that the company was uniquely qualified to support its target customer's current and future needs. This customer proposition is supported by the Brand Territory—an ecosystem that Quest Manufacturing builds with each customer by understanding their needs beyond the immediate requirements of a contract. This is possible because of the Brand Core, the company's instinct for collaboration. Supporting the customer proposition, and rooted in the Brand Core, are four pillars or brand attributes: robust processes, domain expertise, demonstrated vision and strategy, and competent leadership and staff. We were now ready to create the brand identity.

ideantity™

ideantity is chlorophyll's trademarked entity to expresses brand identity. It is the combination of a brand name, the logo, and the tag line.

Think of ideantity as a one-second advertisement. A logo by itself can be impressive but it does not tell the whole story. But a logo and a tagline together, and the way they are presented, can convey a complete story of a company at a glance. It's a powerful way to announce who you are and what you stand for.

Coming up with a name is both exciting and frustrating. For one, it's almost impossible to satisfy everyone. Second, it is increasingly hard to come up with names that are memorable, meaningful, available for trademark, and available as a website URL.

We started with a long list of 300 names and had to eliminate most of them for one or more reasons, presented the client with a short list of fourteen names that they extensively debated, and finally settled on one name that everyone liked and agreed on.

AEQUS
ecosystems of efficiency

Aequs. Pronounced *ay-cus*. The word *Aequs* is derived from the Latin *aequus*, meaning equal. It reflects how the company views its stakeholders and also reflects their approach to growing the manufacturing business through efficient, global ecosystems.

The Aequs ideantity comprises two parts: a visual comprising two parallel strokes at the bottom of the letter Q in Aequs that reflect a sense of collaboration and concerted efforts; and a brand line 'ecosystems of efficiency' that completes the communication.

Aravind summed up the engagement thus: 'I'm glad we went through the exercise in such detail,' he said. 'Over the six months that it took us to create this brand, we were forced to examine our core beliefs and how we want to grow as a company. We now have clarity on the way forward.'

Aravind was clear that his values—trust, respect, and transparency, must be institutionalized and so we worked with the head of HR and heads of departments to ensure that every employee right down to the worker on the shop floor understood three aspects: how these values translated into day-to-day behavior; how they would be deterred or rewarded if their behavior was not aligned; and what to do if you found your own boss was not aligned! This last bit is critical in a hierarchical society like India.

We converted the suggestions into a booklet in Kannada and English that everyone could carry. To us at chlorophyll, the truth of a brand is best expressed in its behaviour (both internal and external) and not just in its communication. In this age of information overload, the most trusted sources of communication are peer group opinions.

The chlorophyll approach to branding

Let's now move from the specifics to the general. From the start we were clear that chlorophyll was a brand consultancy and not an advertising or communication agency. So we developed processes to immerse ourselves in how the brand owners saw the future of their businesses. We made it mandatory for the senior-most clients to attend and provide us time out of their offices, undisturbed by phone calls. And because a brand is an idea, we built into the process small interventions that made tangible the intangible concepts. For example, before we discussed the non-financial measures of success, we requested all the members to hand over their wallets to us. The momentary hesitation of parting with what they believed was of value drove home the point that there was something of greater value that they needed to focus on.

Because brand thinking involves every single department of a company, we built into the process inclusiveness at all levels. We made sure employees who were not part of that off-site immersion session were heard. We made sure all departments had the opportunity to comment on the direction the brand was taking.

Because we as Indians tend to be less open about our opinions in from of our superiors, we even built in cocktails. A couple of drinks helps people speak their minds!

We kept fine-tuning the process. For several years it was a meandering diagram that mixed up client interactions as well as chlorophyll internal steps. We disciplined it down to six; then a few years ago, added back two more.

Creative process versus strategy process

There is a flawed belief that the creative process is divergent and lateral. It is *not*. Any creative process used for solving a problem (as opposed to self-expression) involves waves of convergence and divergence.

That is the insight that became the basis of the chlorophyll process; the eight steps are actually creative steps, where we explore options, then narrow them down, and repeat. That is how we have a process for every single output—for creating the brand strategy; for creating brand names; for creating brand identities; for aligning behaviour to values, whether customer or employee; for creating brand experiences; for creating metrics; for deciding brand architecture.

The model innovation

One of our early learnings was that all discussion around brands happened through the lens of communication. When we interrogated multiple models, we realized they came up short on three counts:

One: almost all brand models focused on consumer brands. There was very little guidance on corporate brands or service brands.

Two: almost all brand models focused on brand communication. There was very little guidance on brand behavior, which is critical for service brands.

Three: almost all brand models focused on conventional competitors; while in reality most competition happened against brands from unrelated categories.

Therefore, we invented our own brand model called anthrop™ and started applying it to the product and service brands we were working on. In 1999, we committed ourselves to the idea of an ideantity, defined as a 10-second ad instead of a logo. Over the years, we have created over 100 of these.

In 2003, Anand Halve invented a tool to define and differentiate corporate brands. It won us the Infosys Employer brand assignment. In 2007, we invented a new model for brand experience. In 2010, we invented litmosi™, a tool for CEOs to understand the alignment (or lack of) of employee behaviour to values. In 2014, we re-adjusted the existing process to deepen employee engagement in organizations.

The HR innovation

An ad agency head who attended the launch of chlorophyll commented that chlorophyll would not survive because there were too many big egos in one small room. That prediction was made in 1999; seventeen years have passed.

There are several reasons we survived and thrived.

One: none of us had ambitions of becoming multi-millionaires. We were aware we needed to grow, but beyond that generic need of any business, we did not submit to extremely aggressive financial objectives.

Two: we were not obsessed about competitors. For the first five years, we saw our role as educating partners about the whole branding process and finding new ways of making that work.

Three: we did not change our salary structures, and thus kept the working capital needs low. When we made a profit, we shared it.

Over time, almost all our energy was devoted to embracing change within chlorophyll rather than worrying about the outside world: when the relationships between brands and stakeholders started changing due to the internet and the rise of social media, we invested in learning from the best in the world in workshops in Singapore or London. When brand experience design became critical to service brands, we invested in learning from Dr Yeoh Teng

Kwong's workshops; he is the person who trained the legendary Singapore Airlines service.

Self-referential integrity

Everyone agrees that 'a brand is what a brand does.' We agree and apply this rule to ourselves from our brand name to our identity to our own models and to our processes. We are now on the verge of re-inventing ourselves to incorporate new disciplines in innovation.

Quintillion Media

Quintillion Media Pvt Ltd owns and runs *The Quint*, a digital newsmagazine like Buzzfeed or Huffington Post for the 'mobile-first, social-native consumer'. Quintillion is also the majority shareholder in *Bloomberg Quint*, a business and financial news joint venture.

The force behind Quintillion is Raghav Bahl and his wife Ritu Kapur. In 2014, Bahl exited from Network18, a company he founded in 1993 with Rs 50,000 and grew to becoming one of India's largest media giants that runs online properties IBNlive.com, Moneycontrol.com, Firstpost.com, Cricketnext, Homeshop18, bookmyshow.com, and TV channels such as Colors, CNBC TV18, CNN-IBN, IBN7, and CNBC Awaaz. The unbridled expansion was funded through borrowing and by the end of 2011, Network18 had accumulated Rs 1400 core of debt and had become unviable. Help came from Mukesh Ambani's Reliance Industries Ltd which invested in the company indirectly in 2012 through debentures convertible to shares anytime within ten years. Two and a half years later, Reliance converted the debentures and took complete control of Network18. Bahl exited with a reported payout of Rs 700 crore.

In 2015, Bahl used a part of that money to start two different but complementary startups: Quintillion Media, a content company, and Quintype, a technology company that develops and markets a digital publishing platform—a kind of a next gen Wordpress.

So Bahl is now a newsman who not only owns his content but also owns the media and the technology that delivers it. In a country where the media is increasingly being owned and controlled by business and political interests, this is good news.

'*The Quint* is not the only independent digital media property,' says Sevanti Ninan, founder and editor of media watchdog *The Hoot*. 'Others like *scroll.in* and *thewire.in* also operate in that space. But *The Quint* is better resourced and better capitalized than any of them. Combine that with Raghav's experience in building news media and the lessons he has learned, and he is very well placed to succeed as an independent media entity.'

In many ways then, Raghav Bahl (born 1960), an engaging conversationalist with a brisk and pleasant manner, alumnus of St Stephen's College and an MBA from the Faculty of Management Studies, Delhi, is on an interesting second startup journey. This is his story.

Leader speak: Raghav Bahl

After I exited Network18, I could have turned angel investor and played golf. But that is not me. I also had this strong feeling that I had sold myself short the first time around and wanted to do it all over again, this time without committing the mistakes I made then.

When you are a first generation entrepreneur you don't really understand the full implications of what you do. It's easy to get carried away by the excitement of building the business. We ended up not having the balance sheet strength to support our ambitions.

That would not have been disastrous in many other industries. Many of the IT, pharma, and other giants you see today have been built by first generation entrepreneurs who could fund their growth plans by progressively diluting promoter equity in exchange for successive rounds of capital.

What did me in was a draconian government rule that made it compulsory for the promoter in a TV news broadcast company in India to maintain 51 per cent ownership at all times. In hindsight, that was the bullet that killed us.

We went from 100 crore rupees revenue in 2005 to about 6,000 crore rupees in 2014. We grew so much so fast that we started challenging industry leaders like Zee that had grown over twenty-five years. But the 51 per cent ownership clause meant that for every rupee someone else put in the company, I had to match it with a rupee of my own. So I was always in debt and that turned out to be debilitating. You can't manage a weak balance sheet. The only way to come out of it is to either dilute aggressively or sell. Since we couldn't dilute, I sold.

So I exited and emerged with a much better capitalized personal balance sheet—something I never had previously. I was now better prepared to start all over again. The balance sheet constraint wasn't there, the learnings were.

The Quint

So that's why we started *The Quint*. Print, of course, is dying. Television requires scale, and in any case, the business has consolidated. We had built thirty-five TV channels from scratch at Network18 and they continue. Zee has forty TV channels, Star has forty TV channels. The top four or five networks control 80 per cent of the market.

But digital was exciting because it was disruptive. Digital also excited me personally because it was a chance to learn something new. At Network18 we had built a good digital business, but I wasn't hands-on then, I was more a strategy person there. So *The Quint* was an opportunity to build something from the scratch.

I don't think we are doing anything particularly new in terms of content. We develop content that is relatively short, more visual, and more youthful compared to traditional media and that gives us a strong connection to our audience. But legacy media have the one thing that startups like us don't have: existing market share. If they can graft new ideas to their existing market share, they can have a good thing going.

So we have to think differently. *The Quint* that you see today is only ten per cent of what it can be. There is so much more potential.

One of the things we plan to do is go deep into verticals. Today we cover a lot of areas. We cover politics, sports, entertainment, health, technology, social web culture, and what have you. At some point we will start going deep into some verticals.

The other big insight we've had over recent months is that the future of content is a mix of digital and television. But—and this is important—the challenge is to repurpose television content, which is a linear and sequential medium, to the non-linear, time-shifted way that content is consumed on the web.

Let me explain. When the news breaks, the first port of call is television. Television will do a complete 360-degree coverage of what's happening: reportage, analysis, live video, drone cameras, talking heads, all of it. It can also incorporate social media content that people start putting up on the net immediately after an event.

So if digital is just going to be a dump of what's happening on TV, it's going to lose the plot. Instead, digital must differentiate through instant crowd sourcing for text and video content, provide immediate analyses and perspectives, dig into history, and provide that instant last mile connectivity that TV cannot match. TV requires time to generate and disseminate content and it can only show one thing at a time. On the internet, you can open multiple windows simultaneously, hyperlink extensively, and provide each viewer with perspectives relevant to him or her.

Some of this is happening already. A good international example would be cnn.com and an Indian example would be ndtv.com.

Our joint venture *Bloomberg Quint* combines both our beliefs—that media companies would need to go deep vertically, and would need to integrate TV and digital. *Bloomberg Quint* is a digital media property that that has a vertical focus (business), combines text and video content, and is a possible template for our future. One of my strengths was in forging partnerships and I see no reason why we should not develop many more partnerships as we explore other verticals.

Quintype

Creating a compelling TV plus digital news medium requires a strong technology platform. And that is where Quintype, our technology startup comes in.

Television technology is fairly simple. You produce something, you uplink it, it gets bounced off a satellite, you downlink through a box, send it into households, and that's it.

But digital is not just content; it's also a lot of technology. In digital, you are in a one to one conversation with the consumer. The consumer can write back to you, can talk to you. And this means that you can map the consumers' habits and predilections. To leverage this very active, intelligent two-way transmission of content, you need a strong technology platform that can understand your consumers and enable you to personalize your offering.

That kind of capability requires not just content generation and dissemination capability but also significant big data analytics capability.

That's why we set up Quintype. When we started *The Quint*, we had two options: offer it on a third-party platform such as WordPress or Drupal, or build our own platform.

We took the longer and tougher route of building our own platform. Quintype is co-founded by me and a Silicon Valley based entrepreneur and now has about fifty engineers based in Bengaluru and California. We've combined our experience in the media and the technical smarts of a very bright team of engineers to build a platform that any digital publishing company will find compelling. The platform has algorithms to monitor audience behaviour and tastes, and to serve personalized content depending on their habits and predilections.

But—and this is where you need to make a judgment call—you need to be careful not to go overboard on technology. For example, based on a reader's stated preferences and reading habits, the algorithm can determine that you like cricket and Bollywood. But we would be very stupid if we then offered the reader a newsfeed based on that cohort or even its complementary cohorts such as other sports or entertainment and some political and business news.

Because that's not how people consume news. Sure, people have likes and preferences but as a reader, you also depend on serendipity to read news that you stumble upon at random. You enjoy the discovery.

That's the eternal challenge in any media organization and digital doesn't change that. You cannot be hidebound. There will always be a need for an editor to make judgment calls and curate a newsfeed.

What digital does is to enable a level of personalization that was not possible in conventional print or television media. It boils down to this.

Technology is changing the way people consume media and as internet connectivity and smartphone penetration improves, more and more people will get comfortable with, and demand, high quality, non-linear, personalized newsfeeds.

But the need for high quality editorial judgment will never go away. In an era where we are bombarded with unfiltered information through social media and slanted news, people still crave for the authority of a *New York Times* or a BBC for authenticity.

The challenge for any media organization is to understand and use digital technology intelligently. We need to balance the siren call of big data and analytics driven algorithmic programming with its promise of delivering personalized content with the old fashioned judgment calls that editors need to make day in and day out.

The Quint is an experiment towards that goal.

Team Indus

Team Indus is the only Indian team participating in the Google Lunar XPRIZE, a competition open to everyone around the world. To win, a privately funded team must be the first to: one, successfully place a spacecraft on the moon's surface; second, travel 500 metres; and third, transmit high-definition video and images back to earth.

The first team that successfully completes the mission will win $20 million; the second team will win $5 million. Teams must prove that 90 per cent of their mission costs were funded by private sources. All teams had until the end of 2016 to announce a launch contract and they have to complete their mission by the end of 2017. There are additional prizes for achieving set milestones. The judges are internationally recognized space technologists and administrators.

Sixteen teams from around the world are in the fray: three from the USA, three international consortiums, and one each from Israel, Italy, Malaysia, Japan, Germany, Hungary, Brazil, Canada, Chile, and India.

Team Indus from India is building a 600-kilogram spacecraft that will be launched by an ISRO (Indian Space Research Organization) rocket. The spacecraft will carry a ten-kilogram four-wheel drive rover equipped with cameras to beam back images and video.

Team Indus is the brainchild of Axiom Research Labs, a technology startup headed by Rahul Narayan, an Indian Institute of Technology Delhi alumnus. The venture is partly funded by private donors but is looking for sponsorships and donations on a large scale to finance the cost of the $75 million moon shot.

This first person account is based on a visit to the Team Indus facility and conversations with team members Sheelika Ravishankar,

Ananth Ramesh, and others. With Star Wars inspired titles like Jedi Master and Skywalker, Team Indus in their simple facility near the Jakkur airstrip in Bengaluru is much more than a technology demonstrator. It is an incredible adventure.

Team speak

We were late entrants to the Google Lunar XPRIZE competition. We registered the team at the end of 2010 and it was an impulsive decision. We had no plan in place and even struggled to come up with the $50,000 needed for registration. For the next one year, nothing much happened. I think we were still shell shocked at what we had done. We had no team in place, we had no financing in place—nothing. It was just a bunch of guys with a dream.

By 2012, we got serious. Rahul Narayan, who started it all, was based in Delhi at that time and soon realized that for anything related to space in India, we had to be in Bengaluru since that is where everyone to do anything with space research was. We initially received a lot of help and encouragement from the National Aerospace Laboratory and even worked out of their guesthouse for the first couple of months before moving to our present leased property in Jakkur.

The team grew slowly. Initially there was only Rahul and about ten others and they have been through some tough times as we struggled with no money and very little support. We are about ninety strong now—mostly young scientists and engineers guided and mentored by a group of retired space scientists from ISRO.

It's an amazing team. The people who join know this is not just another job. Only three countries in the world have ever put a spacecraft on the moon: USA, Russia, and China. If we succeed, it will be a first for India. In 2008, ISRO successfully launched *Chandrayan*, a lunar probe that orbited the moon and even crash landed a probe on its surface. But that was only a probe and is not comparable to the soft landing that we plan with our moon rover.

The rules of the competition state that a team can use any agency to launch their spacecraft. The challenge is to land it on the moon, drive it for half a kilometre, and send back pictures and video. We will be using ISRO's Polar Satellite Launch Vehicle (PSLV) to launch our spacecraft in late 2017.

Twelve minutes from launch, the spacecraft will be in an elliptical orbit around the earth with a perigee (nearest point) of 880 km and an apogee (farthest point) of 70,000 km. The spacecraft will then orbit the earth two and half times, raising the apogee by 10,000 km each time by firing the thrusters on the spacecraft. This manoeuvre is called the trans-lunar injection and will help the spacecraft to escape earth's gravity and send it on its way to the moon.

The spacecraft will reach a peak speed of 10.3 kilometres per second and will take seven and half days to reach within 100 km of the moon. It will then decelerate to be ready for what is called the lunar orbit capture. This is a complicated manoeuvre which will result in the spacecraft being caught by the moon's gravity. The thrusters on the spacecraft are then fired to decelerate while orbiting the moon, getting closer to the lunar surface every time.

Landing is the tricky part. Since there will be no time for signals to traverse to and from the command centre on earth, the landing is completely autonomous and will be controlled by software on board the spacecraft using data collected from laser sensors to guide the spacecraft as it decelerates and descends. The landing site will be Mare Imbrium (Sea of Showers), a vast dusty area on the moon. The spacecraft is scheduled to land at the break of the lunar dawn to help make the most of the lunar day. Once the spacecraft lands, we will establish contact with earth, deploy the rover, and beam back high definition lunar images.

There are several variables in the journey. Depending on where the PSLV leaves the spacecraft, and depending on when it is captured by the moon's gravity, the total time will be between ten to fourteen days to travel the 384,000 kilometres to the moon. And the lighter our spacecraft, the farther the PSLV can propel us from earth.

As of now, our spacecraft weighs less than 600 kg including a lander of 60 kg and a rover of 10 kg. The propulsion system, needed to manoeuvre the spacecraft after the PSLV leaves us in the geostationary transfer orbit, weighs about 400 kg. The balance is made up of subsystems like thermal implementation, power, electronics, and navigation sensors.

We are working on reducing the weight of the lander because every kilo saved gives us the opportunity to add a commercial payload. It's been forty-five years since anyone landed a commercial payload on the moon and there is huge interest from universities, research laboratories, and corporations from around the world to send their instruments with us to obtain a lunar sample or conduct an experiment on the lunar surface.

As of now, we can accommodate a commercial payload of 10 kg. We are working on increasing that because the commercial payload is one of our most important sponsorship opportunities. The total cost of the mission is around $75 million and we need to generate a large part of it still. There are several sponsorship opportunities open to individuals and organizations ranging from printing your name on the spacecraft, to contests for payload experiments, to outright donations. The rules of the contest are that 90 per cent of the cost should be privately funded and so we are keen on attracting as many sponsors as possible.

One of the ways in which we have validated our design and capability is by winning a Milestone Prize. There are milestone prizes where competing teams can put up their design for scrutiny in three categories: landing technology, imaging technology, and locomotion technology. We won a $1 million milestone prize for demonstrating that our lander could survive the vibrations during its launch from earth on the PSLV and during impact on the moon during the landing.

Putting a lander on the moon is a new thing even for the retired ISRO scientists on our team. No one in India has done it before.

We face many challenges. One, the landing will be completely autonomous. It will take two and a half seconds for a signal to travel up and down from the mission control in Bengaluru to the spacecraft while landing on the moon. That is too long for any course correction. So the last fifteen minutes of the landing sequence will need to be entirely preprogrammed and will have to execute flawlessly.

Two, the variable thrust engine technology that is used by Western space agencies to control the descent of the lander is not available to us. So we are using an alternative approach that works by deploying a set of sixteen thrusters that will be controlled by pre-programmed software to switch on and off to control the descent.

Three, the rover has been a huge challenge. The rovers that have gone to the moon till now have weighed 150 kg or more. Our vehicle just weighs 10 kg and is the size of a children's tricycle. Keeping such a light object stable and rolling on the moon presents unique challenges. Firstly, the moon has one-sixth the gravity of earth and so the rover would be that much lighter on the moon. Secondly, the moon's surface is covered in fine sand that is extremely abrasive. Designing a vehicle that can travel 500 metres on such a surface involves designing special wheels to have traction on the lunar surface and accommodating power, motion control, camera, and communication subsystems.

The Team Indus project has been one of continuous learning and innovation. We are building one of the lightest, most efficient, and cost effective lunar landing spacecrafts in the world. In the process, our engineers have had to grapple with availability, performance, and interoperability of subsystems while keeping power and fuel consumption low. While we did start off by attempting to assemble off-the-shelf components, that has not always worked. At this point, the flight computer, dual gimbal mechanism, power control modules, antennas and the spacecraft structure have all been custom built in-house. In the process, we have developed significant intellectual property.

The spacecraft dynamics and its control algorithms are custom designed and are being continuously refined through thousands of simulations to prepare for the remote landing. The last fifteen minutes before touchdown on the lunar surface is a completely autonomous manoeuvre and preparing for this is especially challenging. This is the trickiest part of the mission as it cannot be tested on earth before flight.

The only reason we have been able to do all of this is because of an extraordinarily committed and motivated team. Take for instance the rush to build the prototype for the Milestone prize. Someone in the leadership team took ownership and drove the project to completion in 100 days. Several team members virtually lived in the office during that time.

Our engineers and scientists come from a wide range of backgrounds. People have joined fresh out of college; others have left lucrative jobs in corporate India to be part of the dream. And of course, nothing would have been possible without the knowledge and guidance of our team of retired scientists and engineers from ISRO who have chosen to plunge into yet another space mission, but this time without the comfort of a large organization behind them.

So what of the future? If we succeed in putting our lander and rover on the moon, it will be a huge win for us and for India. By the time we launch, we will have developed a formidable body of technology and skills in designing, assembling, and launching low cost spacecrafts and payloads into orbit. That could result in a valid business proposition to launch satellites or drones. And even, if for any reason, the mission does not go 100 per cent as planned, those lessons, technologies, and skill sets would still be invaluable.

We travel in hope.

Epilogue

One of the fascinating things about researching this book was to discover the many different ways in which business leaders have built their companies.

Can vision be institutionalized? Leaders like Ratan Tata, N R Narayanamurthy, and Suresh Krishna believe it can be if you hire the right people and train them well. Others like William Bissell, Kiran Mazumdar Shaw, and Meraj Manal are convinced that only a founder can make bold bets and see them through.

Can companies effectively balance their social responsibility and shareholder expectations? Dr Devi Shetty seems to be doing that successfully at Narayana Hospitals, a listed company. Others like the Tata group are finding it difficult to strike that balance as investors clamour for better performance.

Can innovation be built into business planning and processes? Companies like GE have done this repeatedly and have reinvented themselves again and again over their 100 plus years of existence. But Indian conglomerates are struggling to achieve the same nimbleness.

Many of these questions have no definitive answers. And why should they? There are many roads to the top of the mountain. Who is to say which one is better?

Appendix

Innovation stories—personal examples

Ramco Systems

In 2000, I headed communications at Ramco Systems, the Chennai based enterprise software company. One afternoon, the founder and CEO, P R Venketrama Raja, a soft-spoken technophile with an MBA from the University of Michigan, strolled in. He wanted ideas for naming his pet project at that time—a software platform that had been developed in-house and for which he had great hopes.

Names are subjective things and so I have a standard approach to them. 'What kind of names do you like?' I asked him. 'Software product names certainly, but anything else too. That may help trigger ideas.'

'I really like *DreamWorks*, Steven Spielberg's name for his company,' he mused. 'It seems to describe exactly what I want to convey about our software platform. It's imaginative and creative but it's also solidly practical.' [DreamWorks has subsequently changed ownership.]

'There's a standard tactic in naming,' I said. 'When you juxtapose opposites, you get powerful imagery. Dark and light. Yin and yang.'

'Give me an example,' he said.

'Firewater,' I said. 'It's what the Native Americans are supposed to have called alcohol. It both ignites and quenches.'

'That's actually pretty good,' he said. 'Let me think about it.'

I left Ramco soon after that and haven't met PRV since. I'm sure there was a formal process involving marketing people, creative agencies, and other stakeholders before the name was finalized.

But the name that finally emerged was VirtualWorks. A juxtaposition of the imagined and the real.

I like to think I played a part in its genesis.

Progeon

In 2006, I headed marketing at Progeon (later renamed Infosys BPO), the business process outsourcing subsidiary of the Indian software giant, Infosys. Akshaya Bhargava, the limerick-writing, Indian Institute of Management Calcutta educated CEO of Progeon wanted a strong story to differentiate the company from the competition. He decided to position Progeon as the transformation BPO.

Transformation is a terrible cliché in the business world. Companies are quick to hype every little thing as transformative and customers and analysts are quick to laugh at such claims.

So Akshaya decided to define transformation in a way that would appeal to his potential customers—large organizations looking to cut costs and improve efficiency. He described transformation as a four-step process with quantifiable benefits at every step: do it cheaper; do it better; do it differently; and eliminate (some) work.

'Our transformation promise was that if we start with a 100 people at the client, we had a roadmap to cut that by a significant percentage over time if the client gave us interconnected processes', said Akshaya. 'We would use a combination of process excellence, domain knowledge, and technology interventions to deliver the same or better output more efficiently.'

This was a fairly revolutionary idea at the time because it directly impacted the way BPO companies made money. The BPO industry worked on the basis of FTEs or full time equivalent. Simply put, it lifted and shifted business processes from high-cost locations to low-cost locations and billed customers for the people-hours of effort.

Our transformation promise knocked this revenue model on its head. Replacing a 100 people at the customer site with, say 60 people at the BPO site was great for the customer but meant lower billing for the BPO. To counter the loss, we would have to do something even more revolutionary—convince the customer to share a part of their gains resulting from outsourcing. Later, this would come to be known as outcome based pricing.

To make the promise credible, Akshaya needed real-life examples. So we ran an internal competition asking business groups to map their customer engagements to the four-step transformation framework. Then armed with the story, we went to market with our transformation promise. Customers were pleased to see a tangible roadmap for their outsourcing plans. Analysts and investors were intrigued by our message. Business, and our reputation, boomed.

About The Author

Vijay Menon is a Bengaluru based marketing and communication consultant. He helps organizations to tell their story better. Vijay has previously worked as a marketing leader in the IT industry, as a journalist with *India Today*, and as a nuclear engineer. He holds an M.Tech. from the Indian Institute of Technology Kanpur, and has attended the Duke-Infosys executive program.

For more information, please visit www.vijaymenon.com.

www.ingramcontent.com/pod-product-compliance
Ingram Content Group UK Ltd.
Pitfield, Milton Keynes, MK11 3LW, UK
UKHW041314190726
13845UKWH00025B/250

9 789386 432698